Dangerous Law Practice Myths, Lies and Stupidity

Judd Kessler
Gunter Enz
Michael Quade
Lawrence Kohn
Albert Barsocchini
Thomas Hauck
Brian Whitaker

FORTUNE HOUSE
PUBLISHERS

Dedication

This book is dedicated to all of our employees and associates who together have cheerfully and tirelessly helped hundreds of thousands of lawyers create the law practices of their dreams, and to those lawyers and their clients for giving us the opportunity to serve them. They have all shared with us these myths, lies and stupid things they were told to do so we can examine them here and make sure that they don't have to recur.

Forum

Visit www.lawmyths.com to add your two cents.

Environmentally Aware Publishing

This book saved 20 pages by eschewing the publishing tradition of adding blank pages to have all chapters start on right-hand pages.

Table of Contents

INTRODUCTION

You worked hard getting through law school. You're working harder as an attorney devoted to your law practice. You serve your clients with sincerity and high ethical standards. So your success is guaranteed, right? Maybe, until something unexpected bites you.

Whether you're fresh out of law school hanging your first shingle, or you've been practicing law since judges wore powdered wigs, your greatest enemy is pointless orthodoxy: habits that have long since lost their usefulness; tasks done by rote; systems and practices that were outdated years ago. Myths, lies and stupidity infect the law profession like fungus in a high school locker room. They sap your energy, create chaos, cost you money and prestige, and make it harder for you to succeed.

Recommended technology from just ten years ago is now dangerously out of date and can put your firm at serious risk. Newer technologies including email, the Internet, and video are often incompatible with older technologies. Clients, insurers, bar associations, vendors, and courts are increasingly demanding the use of current technology and malpractice insurers have stiffened their penalties for inadequate technology adoption.

What career-crippling blunders are being made by otherwise perfectly intelligent lawyers? With advice from lawyers who are in the trenches every day, running small practices and large law firms, in cities and in the country, in nearly every area of practice, you'll discover what their hard-won experience has taught them so that you don't have to make the same mistakes.

You'll learn from parables featuring our fictional law practice guru Arthur Simon, Esq. as he mentors lawyers facing circumstances exactly like you're certain to face.

Each chapter of this informative and entertaining book presents one-easy-to-read Law Practice Myth and shows you how these commonly held beliefs can befuddle, obstruct, and even destroy your law practice. Through Arthur's wise counsel you'll learn the positive steps you can take to avoid disaster and make your practice the envy of your colleagues.

Judd Kessler

1: The Two-Calendar Myth

Keeping one calendar is good, keeping two is better

Dick Scott was a gifted child. His parents recognized very early that he was destined for greatness. He skipped a grade in high school, got a full scholarship to a top local law school, graduated *summa cum laude*, and won the top new associate position at one of the most prestigious law firms in his state. He learned the ropes and was soon hired away by a specialty boutique firm. Having practiced for five years he and a colleague are opening their own firm, Scott & Billings, PC.

Arthur Simon has been a friend of and mentor to Dick since the day Arthur was a guest lecturer on Civil Procedure at Dick's law school. Arthur immediately recognized the qualities in Dick that would make him a fine lawyer.

One day Arthur ran into his young friend on the courthouse steps.

"Dick, you look frazzled," said Arthur.

"Tell me about it," replied Dick. "I was late for court because we had a calendar disaster at the office."

"What happened?"

"I needed to find a case file that I knew was on my desk. I've got a lot of folders piled up so I was moving the stacks around. My elbow knocked over my triple mocha latte. Spilled coffee all over the firm's calendar book. Turned a week's appointments into brown soup."

Arthur nodded. "Sounds bad. But of course you had backup."

"Yes, we did! So I ran over to Angie's desk. She got out the backup copy and we opened it up. We looked for this week's appointments. I'll be darned if half of them were wrong! So now I'm yelling at Angie. Turns out she didn't have time to copy the new appointments into the backup copy. We were flying blind. I had to get out my personal appointment book – the one I keep in my briefcase – and reconstruct the calendar. This took a half hour and by the time we were finished I was late for court. I'll be lucky if I don't get sued for malpractice."

Arthur put a hand on his colleague's shoulder. "My friend, it's time. You need to make the change to a computerized calendaring system."

"It sounds complicated," replied Dick.

"It's easier than you think. My eighty-five-year-old father just got his first laptop. He loves it. What's more, you should check with your malpractice carrier. I'll bet you're paying more because you use old-fashioned paper calendars."

The idea of saving money got Dick's attention. "How do these automated calendars work?"

"Ever hear of Brownian motion? It's when all the birds in a flock seem to move together as if they were controlled by one mind. Same with fish – when the shark swims close all the fish move and dart in the same way. Computerized calendaring software does the same thing."

"What do you mean?" Dick asked with a quizzical look on his face.

"The system handles all the deadlines that are set by court rules. So, for example, when you calendar a trial, all the pretrial deadlines like designating experts, posting fees, and motions in limine are automatically calendared for you, completely and accurately."

"What else can it do?"

"Every computer on your network is linked and the data changes all at once. When your calendaring clerk changes any calendar entry, every workstation is updated. All the dates for one case, one client, one attorney, a group, or the entire office are cross-referenced. It even synchronizes with your smart phone."

"How do you check for mistakes?"

"Simple. You print a daily report showing only the calendar entries that changed. You proof it against the source documents. Any errors are noted and corrected. End of story."

"Yeah, but how about security?"

"Security? Like what happens if you spill a drink on your calendar, or lose it somewhere, or your office floods? That's why digital backups, along with paper printouts, provide a level of security unmatched by paper calendars alone."

"It really does everything?"

"Well, not everything," Arthur said with a grin. "You still have to show up on time."

"Sounds good," replied Dick. "Come on, I'll buy you a triple mocha latte."

☑ Simon says: A man with one watch always knows what time it is; a man with two is never sure. Use a computerized calendaring system with one central calendar and everyone will be sure of the calendared events.

2: The Paper Myth
Paper files are the safest and most secure

A visitor entering the law office of Smith & Jones may at first be impressed by what appears to be a beehive of activity. File folders are stacked everywhere – along the walls, on desks, on file cabinets, on top of the microwave in the office kitchen. The young fresh-out-of-career-school staff is busy rummaging through these files, carrying off armloads of folders, poring through reams of yellowed paper.

A door opens and Jane Smith sticks out her head. "Carol!" she calls. "Have you found the Bumstead contract?" From her desk the target of Jane's question peeks meekly from behind a pile of papers that surround her like a fortification. "Not yet," Carol replies. Jane sighs as Arthur enters her office.

"Arthur, this is a disaster," says Jane. "I can't find anything! Yesterday the sewer line out in the street got blocked and all the sewage from everyone uphill backed up into our basement where we keep all of our files. To avoid a disaster we had to get all the files out of the basement and bring them up to the office."

"A very unfortunate situation," said Arthur. "Aside from the plumbing, your real problem is paper. Did you know that paper was invented in the court of the Chinese Emperor Wu as early as the year 140 BCE? We depend upon technology that is two thousand years old. Why? Because we were all taught that paper records are durable, and that a professional law office is first and foremost a library of precious paper documents that represents a hallowed stewardship of contracts, judgments, and correspondence."

Jane nodded. "We save every scrap."

"It cannot be denied that some paper documents are important. Many contracts must be signed by hand, just as they were back in the days of Emperor Wu. Birth certificates and other legal documents still exist on paper. But I follow the Ten Percent Rule."

"What's that?"

"In a typical paper-based law firm such as Smith & Jones, ten percent of the paper in the office consists of critical documents with original signatures or seals that must be preserved. The other ninety percent of the paper files choking the office are totally unnecessary. These should be scanned and stored digitally. Documents containing sensitive information – social security numbers, financial data – must be shredded.

"The advantages are many. With the immense memory capability of today's computers, millions of document files can be stored in a hard drive the size of a paperback book. Digital document files can be backed up in multiple locations, including Internet backup services. Digital files are instantly accessible from the firm's computer workstations or even remotely."

"Here it is!" triumphed Carol as she brought Jane the file. Then her face fell. "It's an old draft." With a sigh she went back to her piles to look some more.

"Jane, there is no reason why you need to spend more than five seconds looking for the Bumstead contract, or any version of it," said Arthur. "With today's technology you can have multiple drafts of a document preserved for future reference. You can find any document by client, matter, or specific words."

"The partners worry that electronic files are less secure than paper files," said Jane. "You know, like if the computers crashed or were attacked by some horrible virus."

"If you want paper as a backup, keep it. That's the belt and suspenders approach," said Arthur. "But which would you rather be sorting through now, those documents from the basement, or the digital versions on your computer?

"Here is a list of the seven principles of the digital office. It's right on your desktop whenever you want to refer to it."

Seven Steps for a Secure Digital Office

1. Don't copy it, scan it. Scan every incoming document.
2. Don't print and file it, link it. Link all documents to related names and matters in your practice management software.
3. Don't store it, shred it. Shred every document that does not include original irreplaceable content.

4. Store original irreplaceable documents in a secure area.
5. Maintain multiple onsite and remote backups of all digital files.
6. Implement appropriate security procedures.
7. Use full text search software so any document can be located in seconds.

"Okay, from now on, we'll start scanning and linking everything so we'll never have to go through this again," promised Jane.

Arthur sighed. Another lawyer was learning a valuable lesson the hard way!

☑ Simon says: Stop handling all that paper! All of the documents in your office should be scanned and linked to clients and cases digitally. Then 90% can be shredded.

3: The Voicemail Myth

An auto-attendant voicemail system improves client satisfaction

Dick Scott stood on the sidewalk gazing thorough the big plate-glass window of the automobile dealer showroom.

"Hey Dick, shopping for a new car?" asked Arthur Simon. He looked through the window and whistled softly. "A new Cadillac CTS would be a nice set of wheels for a junior partner. With the supercharged V8 you'd be able to take off like a rocket."

"Yeah, I wish. With the way things are going I'll be lucky to afford a Corolla."

"Why? I thought business was good."

"We lost a big potential client."

"What happened?"

"We got a call from a private investigator. He had been hired by the movie star Stella Diamond. The PI caught her husband cheating. The guy is a mega-millionaire real estate tycoon. So the PI called us to set up a meeting with Stella."

"Sounds like a great case to work!"

"The private investigator's call went to voicemail. I checked the messages and called him back right away. It couldn't have been more than ten minutes after he phoned. I was too late. He had already set up a meeting with another law firm."

Arthur shook his head. "The race goes to the swift, my friend. Times have changed. You never get a second chance to make a first impression. Every time the phone rings, it is a moment of truth. Will you build good will or ill will? Cold, impersonal, robotic phone systems don't foster warm relations. Answering your phone live whenever possible delights clients. A warm and friendly receptionist can reinforce the client's good judgment to hire you. A frustrating auto-attendant and voicemail system can negate everything good you're doing."

"But if I'm busy answering the phone all day, how will I get any work done?"

"The ideal is for every caller to be greeted on the phone by a live human being that can help them. Many calls are from existing clients who want to know something about their case, like the date, time, or place of something scheduled, or whether a document has been received. With the right technology and training, anyone on your staff can find the answer instantly and satisfy the client."

"That makes sense," said Dick.

"Relatively few calls will be from new prospective clients," continued Arthur. "If you can't be interrupted to take that call, the next best thing is to meet the caller's needs and set the proper expectations. If your receptionist advises the caller that you normally return all calls by 6:00pm and gets the caller's response that they can wait until then, you'll create an opportunity to fulfill a promise and create trust. Of course, if the caller has an emergency that can't wait, you'll have to take the call, or miss the opportunity."

On the sidewalk up ahead Dick and Arthur saw their colleague Liz Lively. She was talking on her cell phone. After a moment she hung up.

"Hey guys, I just landed a new client," she said.

"On the sidewalk?" asked Dick.

"Not exactly. Our phone system can forward calls, messages, and call alerts to my cell phone. I can glance at it and decide how I want to respond. Many times it's nothing urgent. But a few minutes ago the CEO of a big financial services company called the office. The receptionist forwarded the call to my cell phone and I picked up. We talked about his case and we set up a meeting for tomorrow."

"Sounds expensive," said Dick.

"It's not much more expensive than a basic phone system, and when you consider the extra features, it pays for itself," replied Liz. "When I'm commuting, waiting for court, or just not at my desk, I can take and return calls and bill each one when I'm done, right from my phone. For incoming calls I don't take, I get every voicemail message emailed to me as a sound file. I can play it back from my computer and link it to the client and case file. This gives us global recall of all case and client information including phone messages. We also note every incoming or outgoing telephone call, so anyone in the office can review telephone call history and other notes related to the name or matter. For what the system cost, we have saved money and we've become more competitive with the big law firms."

The trio stood in front of the automobile dealership's window.

"Oooh, look at that Cadillac CTS," said Liz. "I think I'll go in and take a test drive. You guys want to come with me?"

"Uh, no thanks," said Dick. "I have an appointment."

"Big client?" asked Liz.

"Something just as important," replied Dick. "I'm going to get our office set up like yours."

☑ Simon says: "Answering your phone is like showing up – it's eighty percent of success." Live answering delights clients. Empower your staff with technology that lets them look up the client and matter and answer most questions instantly. Turn waiting and commuting time into billable time with technology that lets you track and bill for every conversation.

4: The Technology Myth
It's cheaper to run it until it dies than to maintain or upgrade

"Look at this article in the newspaper," said Arthur Simon to his friend Jackson Green, the probate lawyer. The two were seated in the lounge of the University Club, having a drink before dinner. "Here's a guy named Richard Fuchs who owns a 1971 Ford Mustang. He's driven the car over 600,000 miles. Imagine that!"

"How on earth is that possible?"

"Regular inspections and maintenance. Small problems that get fixed never become big problems."

"May I join you?" asked Lionel Jones of Smith & Jones. "I could use a stiff drink."

"Sure, pull up a chair," said Arthur. "What's up?"

Lionel called over the waiter and ordered a double Scotch whiskey. When the drink came he took a swallow and shook his head. "Two days ago we had a server crash at the firm. We just got our systems back up and running. We missed a major client web conference and who knows what else. We lost thousands in revenue and we look like idiots to our big clients. We'll be lucky if we don't get fired or even sued."

"How long has it been since you installed that server?" asked Jackson.

"Oh, it hasn't been that long," replied Lionel. "Perhaps three years ago."

"And when was it last serviced?"

"We never did anything like that," replied Lionel. "The guy who installed it said that we should have him come back every month to maintain it, but we assumed he was just trying to upsell us. We did not sign up for the maintenance service and we thought we made the right decision because nothing ever went wrong."

"Until now," said Arthur.

"Yes, until now. But it's just a cost of doing business. Technologies are changing so quickly that trying to keep up just causes you needless stress. Older technologies are good enough."

"Lionel," began Arthur, "just substitute the word 'laws' for 'technologies' in what you just said and see if that makes any sense to you. Of course you have to keep up with changing laws. Staying current is much less painful than discovering that you need to make big changes because you've fallen so far behind the curve. Have you ever said, 'I can't open that file you sent me because I don't have the latest version of that software,' or, 'Sorry, I can't scan and email that to you, I don't have the technology to do that?'"

Lionel winced. "Yes, I see your point."

Arthur took a sip of his Scotch. "My friend, in the world of computers, three years is an eternity. I wouldn't be surprised if your operating system was compromised because you never installed any of the security updates, your word processing software is so far out of date that you have trouble opening and reading new documents, and you won't be able to reinstall some of your old software on the new server."

"As a matter of fact, we're guilty as charged on all counts," replied Lionel. "Not only that, some of the attorneys in our office got new smart phones that they spent hours trying to sync but it never seemed to work. I didn't realize that it's just because we never bothered with any updates."

"And it's not just a matter of avoiding breakdowns," added Jackson. "The equipment you leased three years ago is probably obsolete. The newer models have faster speeds and more features. The software that is available now is light years ahead of what was on the market three years ago. It's not just the purchase price that matters; you need to consider how much extra billable time you could gain with upgraded technology."

Their first course arrived. "Well, at least good cooking doesn't get obsolete," said Lionel. "I appreciate your advice. Tomorrow I will order a complete review of all of our technology, and we will establish a line item in the annual budget for technology maintenance and upgrades."

☑ Simon says: If you're going to remain competitive, sooner or later you will be buying new technology. It's much smarter to make small upgrades and enjoy the benefits of using the latest technology than to suffer the major expense and turmoil of having to make big technology changes at the worst possible time, when disaster strikes.

5: The Ignorance-Is-Bliss Myth

Notifying clients whenever something happens on their matter makes them uncomfortable

"Don't go near Jane," whispered Carol, the legal assistant at Smith & Jones.

"Why not?" replied Arthur. "It's a perfectly lovely day and I was hoping we could have lunch together."

Carol grimaced. "Don't blame me if she ignores you. She got a difficult phone call this morning and she's been pre-occupied ever since."

"I'll take my chances," smiled Arthur. He knocked on Jane's office door.

"What is it?" said a voice from within.

Arthur opened the door, closed it behind him, and sat down in one of the leather armchairs in front of Jane's big oak desk. "I heard you're having a bad day."

"You could say that," sighed Jane. "Richard Bigbucks was one of my biggest clients. He came in ready to sign the closing papers on the 1031 exchange of a trophy property, a major shopping center. The bank for the buyers sent over some last minute paperwork a couple of days ago, and we took care of it. But it delayed the closing by a couple of days. I didn't tell him about it because we just took care of it and I assumed he didn't need to be bothered."

"And he found out."

"Today when he came in and learned that the final papers hadn't arrived from the bank he went ballistic. He said that he was flying to Rio tomorrow and that this was a terrible disaster. I apologized but he told me that he was seeking other counsel and that I was lucky that he didn't slap me with a malpractice suit."

"Ouch."

"Yeah. His fee was a significant part of this quarter's revenues. Now we're screwed. I'll have to borrow against our line of credit to make payroll."

"You know, Jane, with today's technology, it's not only easy to copy the client with everything that happens on their matter, it makes them want to pay your bills faster because they don't question all the work you've done."

"I suppose you're right. What should I be doing?"

Arthur pulled up his chair. "It's simple: Proper practice protocols prevent malpractice. Any time you change a calendar date on a matter, email the client. Any time you send or receive a document on the matter, attach it to an email to client. Any time anyone has a phone conversation with the client, make a note and email that note to the client."

"It sounds easy enough," said Jane. "If we had this system in place then Richard Bigbucks would still be our client."

"Yes, and he'd be exchanging just his shopping center, not his lawyer, too."

☑ Simon says: The number one cause of malpractice complaints is failure to communicate. Send your clients an email any time something happens on their matter, and attach every document that goes into their files.

6: The Yellow Pad Myth

Using notepads for client meetings, case notes, things to do lists,
phone messages and time records is convenient and efficient

Dick Scott was busy working on a crossword puzzle. "Say Arthur," he said, pencil in hand, "Which Peanuts character has the security blanket?"

"That would be Linus."

"L-I-N-U-S. Five letters. You're right," replied Dick. He sat back in satisfaction. "With your help I have completed the puzzle in record time."

"Glad to be of service."

"Now I have to run. I'm interviewing a witness this afternoon." He rummaged through his briefcase. "Darn! I forgot to bring a legal pad. Do you have an extra?"

"I haven't used a legal pad in years."

"How is that possible? I'd be lost without them. When I interview a client I record my notes on a legal pad. I use legal pads for case notes and things-to-do lists and phone messages. I keep one by my phone to note all my billable time. I use so many yellow legal pads that I order them by the carton, and around my desk they are stacked up like big yellow towers."

"Or like security blankets."

"Hey, come on. There's a big difference."

"Not really. You're relying on technology that was developed back in 1888. A fellow named Thomas Holley at the American Pad and Paper Company first made the pads from cheap leftovers, or sortings, from paper mills. Supposedly the yellow color was chosen because it stimulated the intellect. The rest is history.

"How do you find what you've written?" asked Arthur.

"Easy. I know exactly where everything is. The only time I have a problem is when the cleaning people come through and move stuff."

"Dick, it's time for you to ditch the legal pads. It's costing you lost time looking for notes, extra money to have what you've written interpreted, typed up, and filed, and then you still have to go looking for it. You can skip all of those steps just by using today's technology."

"Really?" inquired Dick.

"That's right," chimed in Sarah Gale, who had just finished reviewing her notes on her digital notepad. She held up her digital notepad.

"If you like to handwrite your notes, it's no problem! My digital notepad reads my notes and converts them into a Word document with the text printed in a standard font. Every note is then linked to the person and matter that it relates to. With just a click, I create a bill slip for that work. And anyone in the office who I need to have see it can get it immediately just by referencing the client or the matter."

"Okay, okay," said Dick. "I'll get rid of my security blankets and start using my computer!"

☑ Simon says: Possession is nine-tenths of the law, and retrieval is nine-tenths of your practice. Although paper and pen is convenient up front, you'll kill yourself retrieving hand written information. Go digital. You'll be glad you did.

7: The Backup Myth

If you back up your data every day you'll be safe

On a fine spring day at the local boatyard Arthur Simon was cleaning up his skiff for the summer season when his friend Oscar McLain came by.

"Say, Oscar, how's that thirty-foot sailboat of yours?" said Arthur. "Are you going to put it into the water this year?"

Oscar shook his head. "My boat is a total loss. As you know, I put it into storage a few years ago. I never looked at it because I assumed that it was safe. This year I wanted to get it out and do some sailing. Yesterday I went to the storage shed and examined the boat and I found that it has become infested with wood-boring beetles. The insects have been tunneling under the epoxy surface and the hull is now so weak that she's unseaworthy. I have no choice but to sell the hardware and burn the hull."

"That's terrible," sympathized Arthur. "Let me buy you lunch and we can commiserate."

They made their way to the Lobster Pool restaurant overlooking the cove, and as they were enjoying fried clams and cold lagers they were joined by Dick Scott.

"Dick, you look rather glum on this lovely afternoon," said Arthur.

"Just when you think you have everything under control, disaster strikes," said Dick.

"What happened?"

"We had a computer problem at the office. We were upgrading to a new server and that's when we discovered it. All of our backups were corrupt."

"How did it go unnoticed?"

"We had ten backup tapes that we would cycle through," said Dick, setting his fried clams platter on the table. "Apparently, our data got corrupted more than ten days ago, and it's data we only look at once a month so nobody noticed it yet. So for the past ten days we've been backing up corrupted data over what was a good backup tape. We wasted hours getting it sorted out."

"Your problem is serious but not uncommon," said Arthur. "What most people forget is that backup systems are like drills. You don't buy a drill because you want a drill. You buy it because you want holes! And you do backups not because you want backups but because you want your data restored!"

"Duh," groaned Dick.

"Yet almost nobody regularly restores data from backups to check its integrity. Here's the rule: Never overwrite a backup until you're sure that the data you are backing up is better than the data you are overwriting. Some data in an office is only accessed monthly. Therefore, if you keep a minimum of sixty separate daily backups before you start overwriting, you'll more than likely discover the corruption or missing data before you start overwriting good backups. Also, make it a practice to once a week restore a file from a backup and verify it works."

"I've learned my lesson," said Dick. "And now, I want to verify that these fried clams are as delicious as they look."

☑ Simon says: Backups are like drills: You don't want a drill, you want holes. You don't want backups, you want good data restored. Use two or more different backup methods daily. Use a web based backup service as well as a separate DVD or tape backups every day. Keep 60 separate daily versions before overwriting. Take today's backup home. At least once a week, restore from the backup and verify something old and something new so you won't be blue.

8: The Hourly Billing Myth
The value of your work is your time multiplied by your rate

Since they were both going to the airport, Arthur Simon and Ismelda Pinto decided to share a cab. When the yellow taxi pulled up to the curb they loaded their bags in the trunk and settled into the back seat. The driver flipped the lever on his meter and the taxi eased into midday traffic.

Twenty minutes later the taxi arrived at the departure gates. The driver switched off the meter. "That will be twenty-five dollars, please," he announced through the dingy Plexiglas divider.

On the sidewalk Ismelda turned to Arthur. "Lawyers and cab drivers having something in common," she said. "We both work with a meter. When the meter is running, we get paid. When the meter is turned off, we don't get paid."

"In that case, the cab driver is getting a much better deal than you are," replied Arthur.

"What do you mean?" said Ismelda. "Charging by the hour is what practically every lawyer does if they're not on a contingency."

With a few minutes to spare before their flight they decided to get a coffee, and were soon sitting at a little table near their gate.

"Billing by the hour may be an easy way for a young lawyer to get a feel for the marketplace," said Arthur. "But you and Charlie Hawley should be far beyond that. I'll bet that you are losing money on many of your cases, and making your clients unhappy in the process."

"How so?" asked Ismelda.

Arthur explained a few of the reasons why charging by the hour doesn't make sense.

1. Don't expect to be paid for more than half of the time you work. You and your staff will spend a lot of time getting ready, organizing, starting, cleaning up, socializing, communicating with each other, learning, training, and a whole lot of other stuff that you can call general and

administrative and shouldn't be billed to clients (unless you want to risk appearing unethical).

2. Forgetting to bill for something or billing less than the time you actually worked is also typical.

3. Clients hate knowing that the meter is running, and being billed for every minute of every conversation makes them reluctant to call you when they need you.

4. When you bill hourly, you can't ethically earn more than the number of hours multiplied by the rate.

5. Regardless of how few or how many hours you spend on a matter, the client has his own concept of the value of your services.

"I understand," said Ismelda. "So what do you recommend?"

"Methods to produce higher revenues include contingency, flat fee, value billing, or creating a product. But have you ever heard of using the blink test?" Arthur said with a wry grin.

"The blink test?"

"Yes, I learned this one from my ophthalmologist. When I went in for glasses I picked out some new titanium frames. When I asked him the price, he said, 'Just three hundred dollars,' and then he paused. When I didn't bat an eye, he continued. 'For the frames. The lenses are a hundred dollars,' and again he paused. I should have learned. When I didn't blink he continued, 'Each.'

"Now I'm not recommending that you quote your fees that way, but the lesson here is that the eye doctor was able to judge the value to me of what he was selling by looking for valuable feedback and responding to it."

"So how do I know what the value of my services are to a particular client?"

"To establish a fair value, you should discuss with the client what his alternatives are if they don't hire you, or if they hire someone else. For example, if a client is being sued for $100,000, if he defaults he stands to lose $100,000. If he hires someone else by the hour and it goes to trial, he stands to lose $100,000 plus attorneys fees and costs. Now say that because of your personal relationship with the attorney for the plaintiff you believe you can settle the matter for $10,000 with just a couple of hours work. Would it be worth a $10,000 fee to the client to have you do that, as opposed to just two hours of billable time?"

"I see what you mean," said Ismelda.

"Even if you don't bill by the hour, you need to keep track of where your time is going to know what cases and activities are most and least profitable. Practice management software is invaluable for that. Every time anyone touches a client, case, or document, she can click a button and log the time. At the end of each month, you can compare revenues collected to the total time expended on each matter."

"Well, Arthur, it looks like it's time I started thinking outside the billable hour box."

"There's no time like the present, Ismelda."

☑ Simon says: Meters are good for taxicabs, but there are better alternatives for a law practice. Use technology to easily keep track of everyone's time as they touch matters, and every month spend a few minutes to analyze the time expended versus the revenues generated per matter.

9: The Low Fee Myth

The less I charge, the more clients I'll get

While walking through the mall on his lunch hour, Arthur saw Jane Smith as she came out of a shoe store. "Find any bargains?" he asked.

"You bet!" she replied. "For only thirty dollars I got a pair of pumps that regularly sell for one hundred dollars!"

"Well, they say that you should never pay full price. How's the firm?"

Jane bit her lip and her expression darkened. "Not good. Something's wrong and I can't put my finger on it. My law school classmate Odell Cochran opened his practice at the same time I did and now his client list is much better than mine. He's got blue-chip corporate accounts and I can't get anything except personal injury stuff and insurance settlements for car crashes. What's particularly galling is that my class rank was above his."

"What does he charge?"

Jane rolled her eyes. "About double what I charge. I don't know how he does it."

They sat on the bench near the gurgling fountain.

"There could be many reasons why Odell is successful. Perhaps he is more aggressive or he markets himself better. His firm may be run more efficiently. But perhaps part of the problem is that you are charging less than you are worth."

"I thought that in a competitive environment, price was important. Just like when I buy shoes."

"People don't hire lawyers the way they shop for shoes. People seek the advice of a lawyer when they face a significant life situation – they are being sued, or they are buying a house, or they have been arrested. If they have the means, they are willing to pay for the best possible legal advice they can get. Tell me, if you had cancer would you rather go to a doctor who drives an old Ford Escort or one who drives a Mercedes?"

"If that's all I knew, I'd go with the Mercedes," said Jane.

"Of course. The doctor who drives the Ford Escort may be a fine physician, but how do you know? To *be* successful sometimes you have to *act* successful."

"But I don't want to cut myself off from less affluent clients who need me."

Arthur smiled. "Those shoes you bought? The designer sold thousands of pairs at one hundred dollars each to people who could afford them. And yet you bought them for thirty."

"Oh, I see!" exclaimed Jane. "I can always discount my fee when I choose. But I can't give discounts unless my fee is high enough."

Arthur nodded. "When clients are faced with life-altering legal issues, they do not want a cut-rate lawyer. They will pay as much as they can afford for the best possible representation."

☑ Simon says: Big checks fix big problems. Don't be afraid to charge what you are worth, and be sure the client agrees that you are worth what you charge.

10: The Website Myth

Just put up a website and they will come

Arthur Simon and Gunter Enz were competing against Oscar McClain and Richard Fry of the law firm McLain & Fry at the Ocean View Golf Club. The 18th hole was a 400-yard par four with a bend in the middle and a broad sand trap lurking behind the green. It requires an initial drive that skirts a clump of tall pine trees on the left. If you get safely beyond the trees you can make par.

Oscar was the last of the foursome to tee up. He hooked his shot directly into the trees. "Blast it!" spat Oscar. "It serves me right. Nothing else is going well either."

"You mean at the firm?" Arthur put his club back in the back.

"Yes. Business has been miserable. We may have to close an office."

They gathered their bags and set off down the fairway. "Don't you have a good website?" asked Arthur.

"Absolutely," replied Oscar. "We just spent a sizeable amount to have a top-notch website." From under the tree he hit his ball down the fairway. It landed in the rough fifty yards from the green.

"Richard and I made a decision to focus all of our marketing efforts on our website. We thought that since this was the new thing, then we should commit one hundred percent. Nowadays everyone finds a lawyer on the Internet, right? So our website is state-of-the-art."

"But nonetheless business is down," said Arthur. He swung and his ball landed just short of the green.

"Sure, but it's just the economy." With a wedge Oscar overshot his ball to the edge of the sand trap beyond the pin.

"Oscar," began Gunter, "How are people finding your website? With millions of sites on the Internet, how are they getting to yours?" With a seven iron Gunter lofted his ball to within two feet of the pin for an easy put in.

Oscar made it onto the green. Arthur, Gunter and Richard made par, and Oscar double-bogeyed. They headed to the clubhouse as the sun was setting over the sail-dotted horizon.

"Gunter, you're the Internet marketing expert," said Arthur. "If Oscar and Richard buy the drinks can you give our friends here a little free advice?"

"I'd be happy to, Arthur. Scotch and soda for me. Boys, having a great web site is a fine start, but it's like a billboard in the desert – who is going to see it? You have to be on a major highway – that is to say, on a successful legal portal, preferably in a premier position.

"Every attorney's information is in some form on the Internet, whether in directories, articles, or bar association disciplinary reports."

Oscar blanched. "I'm just kidding!" continued Gunter. "But it doesn't mean the right potential clients are finding you. You need to bring clients to your website. If you can handle more clients, you should do more marketing. Even if you are busy, are you too busy to take the perfect case? Be prepared. Don't wait for your practice to slow down to get yourself positioned properly."

"How do we bring clients to our website?" Oscar and Richard asked, almost in unison.

"You'll want to advertise on the sites that consumers are going to when they are looking for legal help. These legal portals are spending much more than any single attorney can afford to spend on pay-per-click words on search engines, radio and television ads, and affiliate marketing to bring prospects to the portal. The prospects can then research legal issues and find local attorneys who can help them."

"Why wouldn't we just do the pay-per-click marketing ourselves?" asked Oscar.

"You can certainly do that, if you've got the time and money," continued Gunter. "You may be shocked at how much the keywords cost, and how many clicks it takes before someone sets an appointment with you. What's not obvious is that most non-lawyers are often confused by legal terminology and don't always search online for the right legal terms. They may type in 'I want to patent my logo' because they don't understand the difference between patents and trademarks. The legal portals understand the dynamics of Internet keyword searches. That's their job and they're good at it. And with the combined revenues from the lawyers that use them, they can afford more keywords so they can funnel more of the right clients to your practice than you would get on your own without them."

Oscar and Richard nodded. "You're right!" said Oscar. "We built a big fancy website out in the middle of nowhere. We've got to use the right Internet tools and put up signs to get the traffic we need to succeed."

☑ Simon says: Don't let your website be a billboard in the desert. Put it on a superhighway and drive traffic to it through search engines and law portals.

11: The No Pain, No Gain Myth
To be successful, you need to get out of your comfort zone

At his usual table at Chez Panini, Arthur was enjoying his lunch with Larry Kohn, his close friend who teaches lawyers how to be rainmakers. Seated across the room at a table for two were Jane Smith and a man whom Arthur recognized as J. Cartwright Brontus, a partner at Brontus, Burger, and Stone, one of the oldest general contracting firms in town.

Arthur could not help but notice that it did not take long for Brontus to finish his meal, excuse himself, and leave the restaurant. Jane remained at the table alone. On her face was a stunned expression. Arthur caught her eye and waved her over to his table.

"Hi Jane, you look like you're miserable. Let me cheer you up. Come join us," said Arthur.

Jane slumped in her chair. "I am miserable. A big miserable fool!"

"Why?"

Jane took a sip of water. "It's a long story. But I have always been a firm believer in self-help books. I have them all – the *Pie In The Sky Book*, the *Water and Celery Diet*, the *See The Future* book. To gain more knowledge I recently attended a self-help seminar led by a business guru. The session was six hours long. It was too much information! But one thing stuck in my head. All of us were encouraged to get out of our comfort zones. He said it was the key to success.

"I was determined to take positive action to justify my six hundred dollar investment in the self-help seminar. I thought about ways to promote the firm by getting out of my comfort zone. I remembered that I had met J. Cartwright Brontus at a Chamber of Commerce breakfast. He had given me his business card. I got up the nerve to call him and I invited him to lunch. He accepted. When we sat down I was so nervous that I couldn't eat a thing. He asked me about the firm and I just blubbered something about doing a lot of slip-and-falls. Halfway through lunch I saw him glance at his watch. I felt like a total dingbat and I'm sure he never wants to hear my name again."

Arthur turned to Larry and smiled. "Larry, you've been coaching lawyers to be rainmakers for more than 20 years. What advice would you give to my friend Jane here?"

"Jane, you get an 'A' for effort," said Larry. "You know, most lawyers would have been too uncomfortable to have even made that call to invite Brontus to lunch."

"I get the feeling another shoe is about to drop," said Jane uncomfortably.

"Are you sure you want to know?"

"Yes, yes. Go ahead, I can take it."

"You may have done yourself more harm than you imagine."

Jane looked more shocked and confused than ever. "What do you mean?"

"The negative feelings associated with making that call were strong," Larry continued. "You probably imagined Brontus would think you were being too aggressive or your call was an intrusion. Now, having had a bad outcome, you're going to allow yet one more negative association with rainmaking reinforce your existing distaste for the whole process. That reinforcement stops you from considering other rainmaking activities, which creates a downward negative spiral. Subsequently, rainmaking gets farther and farther away.

"The reality is you should always choose rainmaking activities that are in your comfort zone. For example, if you don't feel comfortable calling a person for lunch, you could think of other, less invasive ways to reach out. Maybe you could invite him to a seminar. Maybe you could send a copy of a recent article as a way of developing a closer connection. Maybe you could call to inquire about the process of getting included on their RFP list. If the feedback is positive, you may feel comfortable making that call for lunch down the road. So, don't buy into the myth of getting outside your comfort zone. Unlike the muscle-building axiom 'No pain – no gain' the rainmaking axiom is 'Fear pain – you'll refrain.' When you stay in your comfort zone, you are much more likely to take action. And if the action is well targeted, there is a greater chance that it will produce the desired results."

"Wow, I never really looked at it that way, and I can see you're right!"

The waiter approached and set down two chocolate mousse desserts. Arthur smiled. "Chocolate releases endorphins. Now let's really get into the comfort zone. Here is your spoon."

☑ Simon says: Fear pain and you'll refrain. Take action within your comfort zone to reinforce your confidence and build your skills by doing what you can do naturally well. Keep track of your efforts by noting every time you reach out to a person, either by phone, email or letter. It's easy with the right technology.

12: The Conflicts Checking Myth

A good paralegal is all you need for conflicts checks

Ismelda Pinto was just taking her seat at the bar association luncheon when she spied Arthur Simon. She waved him over and offered him the seat next to her.

"Ismelda, how wonderful to see you! How is everything at Pinto & Hawley? I read in last month's bar review that you were chosen by Goldfinger Associates to handle their big lawsuit."

"Things are not good," she replied in a low voice. "We had to withdraw. It has become very embarrassing and very costly. I almost called in sick today just to avoid coming to this event."

"Why did you have to withdraw?"

"Before we accepted the case we asked our paralegal Juliet – who has been with us since we started the firm – if she knew of any potential conflicts. She's got a mind like a steel trap. She did the usual checking, including our time and billing software, and she didn't find any conflicts so we thought we were in the clear. But then someone at Goldfinger called and asked about Charlie Hawley's involvement with one of the defendants. Charlie has played golf with him and had helped him pro-bono from time to time with some legal advice, so it seemed inconsequential. Well, it wasn't inconsequential, and the judge was not happy. We're off the case. We spent a couple of hundred hours in preparation and now that's all gone. Getting Goldfinger to pay us is not going to be easy, especially because from their point of view it was one hundred percent our fault."

Arthur nodded as he picked at his salad. "Conflict of interest issues can be expensive. What would you do without Juliet's steel trap memory? Maybe it's time to check into conflict checking software."

"There is such a thing?"

"Absolutely. It is a simple process. You enter every name you want checked, including up to 200 of the prospective adversaries and related parties, and the software scans every name, matter, event and note in seconds. You can even check Social Security numbers. You can search on partial names and do 'sounds like' searches too.

"Once Juliet runs the conflicts check for you, she can print out the report, and you can decide whether any names found are actual conflicts or not."

Ismelda nodded. "We cannot afford to get conflicted out of any more cases. As soon we're done with lunch I'm talking to Charlie about upgrading our conflicts checking systems."

"From Juliet to software," said Arthur. "It's a smart move, and lets Juliet use her considerable skills more productively."

☑ Simon says: Don't rely on someone's memory or limited checking. Be thorough, and use technology designed to find all potential conflicts.

13: The Focus Group Myth

Focus groups are for politicians, not trials

After an evening at the theatre, Arthur retired to the Curtain Call Pub for a late dinner where he joined Michael Quade, who had just finished another jury trial, and Ismelda Pinto, the young criminal defense lawyer.

Over Caesar salad, fish and chips, and a bottle of Chardonnay they discussed the show.

"Wasn't the leading actor just amazing?" said Arthur. "Every line, every nuance of his performance was just perfect. He didn't even seem to be acting – it was all so natural. I believed every word he said."

Michael noticed that Ismelda hadn't eaten much. "Did you enjoy the show?" he asked.

"Oh yes, the play was marvelous," she replied. "I'm just depressed about my day in court."

"What happened?"

"Our defense was solid. We had a witness who placed our guy miles away from the crime scene. I put her on the stand. But for some reason the jury didn't believe her. They found my guy guilty. The prosecutor was so smug as we left the courtroom. He knew his case was flimsy but he won anyway."

"Well, you said the three important words that explain everything," said Michael.

"What are the three words?"

"*For some reason.* You don't know why the jury did not believe your witness?"

"What am I supposed to do? She's not like an actor in a theatre. I can't coach her."

"You are right that she must testify in her own words. But did you ever wonder why Broadway shows always open out of town? The early audiences are like focus groups. They provide feedback on whether different parts of the show are working. They give the director a chance to evaluate the audience response before the show is seen by the New York critics."

Ismelda frowned. "Focus groups for witnesses? Like politicians use? The idea seems phony and vaguely unethical."

"I know how you feel," Arthur chimed in. "But look at it this way: it's your professional obligation to present your case and your witnesses with clarity and empathy. The jury may have an emotional response to your witness that you have not foreseen. Perhaps your witness seems scary or evasive or untrustworthy. You need to know this before you put that person on the stand."

"We represented a client injured in a bar fight," Michael continued. "The defense argument was that our client had started the fight and got what he deserved. After the discovery cutoff, we located a witness who claimed that our client had not started the fight. His testimony should have been a tremendous asset. We gathered some of my friends and office workers for a quick focus group – all it cost me was some pizza and sodas. We discovered that everyone really disliked our witness. They didn't believe him and they thought that he was sleazy and had some ulterior motive. So we didn't call him as a witness and reworked our case to win without him."

"Remember the Kennedy-Nixon debate in 1960?" said Arthur. "Polls indicated that people who heard the debate on the radio scored Nixon higher. People who saw the debate on television thought Kennedy had won. He was more appealing. Nixon may have had a better grasp of the facts, but people just didn't like him."

"Okay, I get it," said Ismelda. "From now on when I have a critical witness, I'll pull together a focus group. We're going to appeal my guy's case and next time we'll do a better job of managing our presentation. Now who wants dessert?"

☑ Simon says: Focus groups give you invaluable insights that can make the difference between winning and losing. Listen to what they deliberate about so you can make it a no-brainer for the trier of fact. Whether you use friends or hire a professional firm to run a mock trial depends on the value of the case, but you should always run your play by an audience off Broadway before you open in front of the real critics – the judge or jury.

14: The Court Forms Myth
Always use forms from the court's website

While strolling through the big marble lobby of the district court building Arthur saw Georgia Billings, the law partner of his colleague Dick Scott. She was seated on a bench with her briefcase perched on her lap, frantically writing on a piece of paper. On the bench beside her were file folders and documents.

"Why hello, Georgia," offered Arthur. He was not sure if she wanted to be bothered because she appeared to be in a great hurry.

"Hi Arthur," she sighed. She put down her pen. "I cannot believe I'm sitting here filling out this application for a writ of attachment. Dick is due in court in five minutes and we've got three more forms to fill out! We had them all filled out, but we used the old forms that my secretary got from the court's website. With the recent budget cuts, the forms on the website didn't get updated and the court won't accept the old ones."

At that moment Dick appeared, breathless from having run inside from the parking lot. "How's it going?" he asked Georgia.

"Almost done. Here, you take this one," and she thrust a document at him. "Fill out all the information about the client and our firm."

For the next few minutes they scribbled furiously. Georgia looked at her watch. "Here, just take what we have. You're due in court now. You know that the judge is a stickler for punctuality."

Dick stuffed the forms into an accordion file and rushed to the big double doors leading into the courtroom. Georgia gathered her papers.

"I think you could use a cup of coffee," said Arthur.

"I sure could!" replied Georgia. "Let's go across the street to Java Joe's."

"You don't need me to tell you that there are thousands of court forms. Petitions, citations, witness forms, proofs, requests for special notices, waivers, attachments, applications, pleadings, family law forms, interrogatories – the list can seem endless."

"Tell me about it," said Georgia as she searched her briefcase for another form.

"How much time do you, Dick and your staff spend filling out court forms?"

Georgia shrugged. "It seems like endless hours."

"And how many mistakes have you made?"

"Too many! We missed a deadline last week because an application to set aside a writ of attachment had the wrong petitioner name. That cost us a bundle."

"What if there was a way that you could have any court form filled out for you with all the information you already had in your files at the push of a button?"

"What, do you have a magic genie in your briefcase?"

"It's like that, but this genie is real. It's part of the practice management software you should be using."

Arthur described what the software can do:

- The forms library organizes your forms into folders based on jurisdiction and case type
- Select any form or group of forms and the program will instantly fill it from your client and matter data
- Type in additional information required on the form, then save, print or e-file your court documents
- Save your preferred standard wording and boxes checked in templates to apply to forms for other similar cases
- Forms stay linked to the matter for fast and easy retrieval

A week later Arthur saw Georgia in the courthouse lobby. She was standing and chatting with a colleague. When Georgia saw Arthur she waved him over.

"You seem very relaxed today," said Arthur.

"We installed the court forms software you recommended," she replied. "It seems like a burden has been lifted from my shoulders. I actually look forward to coming to court."

☑ Simon says: Avoid costly errors and wasted staff time typing information into forms that you've already got on your computer. Automated forms software pays for itself in no time, especially if it's fully integrated into your case management software.

15: The One Big Client Myth
One big client is all you need

At the baseball game Arthur saw his friend Chou Frack of Frick & Frack, LLP. "When I was at the dentist office this morning I happened to pick up a copy of *Yachting Magazine*," Arthur said as a conversation starter. "I saw an advertisement for a rare 1969 Chris Craft 36-foot CC Corvette. It was one of only 34 built, and one of the last wooden boats the company made. It's berthed right here in our harbor. The description reminded me of your boat."

"It *is* my boat." A dark cloud crossed Chou's face.

Arthur admonished himself for his tactless remark, but gently proceeded. "Oh, are you selling it?"

"Yes."

They found seats high in the bleachers where they could talk privately.

"You don't seem happy about selling your Chris Craft," said Arthur.

"I'm not. That boat is my pride and joy. But we've had a crisis at the firm and everyone is cutting back."

"May I ask what happened?"

Chou sighed and took a fistful of Cracker Jack. "A few years ago we started doing some syndication work for a big investment guy. Let's call him 'Bernie.' He was making a fortune and he had more cash than he knew what to do with. He started giving us more and more work. Julie Frick and I discussed what this meant for the firm. We had a choice between keeping the firm lean and focusing our energy on Bernie, or hiring a more people to spread the workload and make it possible for us to keep servicing new clients. We decided to focus on Bernie. Everything was fine until last month. As you may have heard, Bernie went bankrupt and he owes his creditors – including us – millions of dollars."

"So Bernie goes belly-up and you are left holding the bag."

"Yes."

"And now you have to hustle."

"Yes."

"So why are you at a baseball game?"

"I had season tickets. And I needed a break."

"Well, today may be your lucky day. A few hours ago I received a phone call from an old friend. He wanted to hire my firm for a big medical malpractice case. The case looks like a slam dunk, but I had to turn him down because my computer software revealed a conflict of interest. He asked me for a recommendation. I said that I would have someone call him by nine o'clock tonight. Here is his phone number. Call him."

"You bet I will!" replied Chou. He handed the box of Cracker Jack to Arthur and pulled out his cell phone. Within a few minutes he had set up a consultation for the next day.

Arthur dug into the last of the Cracker Jack. He pulled out the toy surprise. It was a tiny plastic boat.

"Here you go," he said as he handed the boat to Chou. "It will be a substitute for your Chris Craft until you can get your career back up to speed."

☑ Simon says: One big client can make you, and just as easily break you. Clients come and go. It's one thing to take that risk as a solo. When you're building a firm where the livelihoods of others depend on your good judgment, remember that there's safety in building a broad client base.

16: The Ivy League Lawyer Myth
The Ivy League lawyer has the advantage

The players were taking the field as Arthur Simon and Michael Quade settled into their seats on the fifty-yard line at the football game. They were soon joined by a young man.

"Hi James!" said Arthur. "Let me introduce you to my friend with the season tickets, Mike Quade. He's a trial lawyer I thought you might enjoy meeting. Mike, this is my nephew, James, who just graduated first in his class from a big Ivy League law school and just hung out his own shingle."

"Nice to meet you, Mike. Hey, it should be a great game. It says here that the quarterback for the home team is a Heisman Trophy winner," said James.

"Do you think that gives him an advantage?" replied Mike.

"What do you mean? I sure think so. It means the guy is going to be a big star. Just like graduating first in the class from the best law school."

"Not so fast, James," said Mike as he dug into his pocket for ten dollars for a beer. "The Heisman Trophy is given to outstanding college football players, but evidence shows that in most cases their success is not replicated in the professional leagues. Consider this: the last time a Heisman Trophy-winning quarterback won a Super Bowl was in 1981, when Jim Plunkett played for the Oakland Raiders. In the past fifty years, scarcely one in five Heisman winners has become a major professional football star. Only four Heisman winners have been voted by the Associated Press as the NFL Most Valuable Player. I could go on, but you get the point."

"Yes I do, but I'm still wondering why?" asked James as he paid for a hot dog and popcorn with a twenty-dollar bill.

"Usually the Heisman winner is selected from the team with the best record, which is hardly an infallible criterion. The NFL defenders are much bigger and tougher than on any school squad. And the rules and play are different when it's for money."

"You're right. I never really looked at it that way. Well, like the Heisman trophy winner, I'm glad to be out of school and in the big leagues. I've already got a great case involving a breach of contract from a college buddy of mine. "

"That's great, James. Whenever I get a new case, I start with the end in mind by checking the jury instructions to see what elements of the case I need to prove to win," said Mike. "Have you done that yet?"

"No, but that's a great idea! Any other tips?"

"Are you planning on video-taping your key witness depositions?"

"No, I think that would be cost prohibitive," said James.

"It may be costly, but the results are often priceless, especially when you see a witness squirming because he's not telling the truth. You just can't see that from the words alone in a printed deposition, but it's glaringly obvious in the video. And when you play it in front of the jury, it can be the difference maker."

"I can see that! Okay, I thought I learned everything I needed to know about trials in law school, but now you've got me a little concerned."

"And you are planning on running some focus groups or a mock trial, aren't you?" asked Mike.

"Uh, I never really considered it. Isn't that expensive?"

"When a case doesn't warrant the expense of a mock trial, I use family and friends for just the cost of some pizza and beers."

"What do you plan on bringing to court with you for the trial?" asked Mike.

"I was going to bring my paralegal who says she'll have everything on a notebook computer," replied James. "She says that's all we'll need."

"Do you really think you're covered?" said Mike. "Computers die. Files get corrupted. You could find yourself up the creek without a paddle. Just like a football team, you need backup. I like to have a trial notebook for each witness, and a complete set of all the documents, indexed."

"Now I'm really worried. I can't believe I didn't think of those things. They seem so obvious now that you've mentioned them."

"James, which would you rather be, the first guy through the mine field, or the second?" asked Mike.

"Okay, I get your point. So how do I bring in an experienced trial lawyer to help me on this first trial?"

"James, I owe a lot to Arthur. He mentored me when I was starting out. I'd be honored to follow in his footsteps and show you how to prepare the case, handle discovery, put together the trial notebooks, manage the trial, deliver the opening and closing, and help you learn and implement the practice protocols to be successful. The key is to anticipate the unexpected. You must have a contingency plan for every possible snafu."

"You're absolutely right," agreed James. "I guess there's no substitute for experience. Here's the kickoff – now with you on my team I can really enjoy the game!"

☑ Simon says: You don't want to be the first one through a minefield. When you don't have experience, get someone on your team who does. It could make the difference between success and failure.

17: The Lead Tracking Myth
Your staff is tracking which of your marketing channels works best

"Roberto, I'd like you to meet my good friend Gunter Enz," said Arthur Simon. "He's in town for a convention and I knew he would enjoy an evening at Chez Panini. And of course you know my colleague Dick Scott."

The rotund owner of Chez Panini smiled and extended his hand and greeted the party seated at the plush banquette under the big oil painting of Roman ruins in Italy. "Any friend of Arthur's is a friend of mine! Welcome!"

"I hear you've been in business a long time," said Gunter. "You must have a lot of steady customers."

"Yes," replied Roberto. "Most of our dinner clientele come from the financial and law offices in the neighborhood. We also have some regulars from the old country, as well as people attending the theatre and the cinema. On weekends we get young people on dates, and in the summer we get tourists from the cruise ships." He smiled knowingly. "I have a special deal with the cruise line. They send me groups and I give them a special menu. Everybody is happy."

"Well, I'm delighted to meet you," said Gunter.

After they had ordered a first course of antipasto with salami, anchovies, olives, roasted garlic, artichoke hearts, pepperoncini, mushrooms, provolone cheese, and pepperoni, Dick raised his glass of Nebbiolo and said, "Here's to surviving one more day!"

"That sounds rather dire," said Arthur.

"I'm just overwhelmed," replied Dick. "Running the firm is getting complicated and our marketing expenses keep rising and I'm not sure if we are getting a good return on our investment."

"How's your client flow?" asked Gunter.

"Okay, I guess, but I'm not sure what's working and what we might be wasting our money on. We have a website, yellow pages, and newspaper ads and I don't know which are worthwhile. So we just keep pouring cash into all of them."

"Not like our friend Roberto, who knows exactly where his customers are coming from," said Gunter. "It's no wonder he is successful."

The waiter appeared and the group ordered dinner and another bottle of the Nebbiolo.

"Gunter," proposed Arthur, "tell my young friend about the high-profile divorce attorney you helped who, like Dick, was frustrated with his marketing."

Gunter explained, "The attorney became a member of an exclusive Internet-based law information marketing service, even though he was skeptical that the Internet could deliver the caliber of clients he wanted. After three months he asked everyone in the office how many leads the service had generated. They only remembered a few calls and didn't think they got any clients.

"Annoyed, he set up a meeting with the director of sales of the marketing service. The director produced a report showing that the attorney had received over 90 calls on the special 800 number they set up to track the calls. After reviewing the report, four calls from the same number over two days, each over ten minutes in length, stood out. When the attorney checked on who the caller was, he exclaimed, 'She just signed a $25,000 retainer with me!' After reviewing more calls on the report, the attorney confirmed two more $5,000 retainers and a $10,000 retainer client.

"That's $45,000 in new business that the attorney had no idea where it came from. He thought everyone in his office was tracking all incoming calls, when in fact nobody was. Luckily the service tracked all email and phone leads through their external system so the attorney was able to see exactly what he was receiving and realized that his ability to track his marketing internally was deficient at best."

"Dick, I think the answer is clear," said Arthur. "Scott & Billings needs a way to track every lead from every source. Your practice management software should make that easy and give you reports telling you where your leads are coming from and your conversion rate. Then you'll have the control over your marketing to get a better return on investment."

At that moment Roberto approached the table. "How is everything?"

"Delizioso!" replied Dick.

☑ Simon says: Track every lead from every source so you can know which of your marketing is working and which isn't. It's just a couple of extra bits of information with the right practice management software and marketing approach.

18: The Rolodex Myth

Everyone in the office should keep their own Rolodex

Emily Silver's cell phone rang. She fumbled in her purse, found the phone, and answered it. After a moment she frowned. "No, I'm sorry, you have the wrong Emily Silver. I do not operate a dog grooming service. No, I do not know her number. Perhaps you should call information. Yes, goodbye." She flipped shut the phone.

"Wrong number?" asked Arthur Simon. He was walking with Emily through the park on the way to the Rotary Club lunch meeting.

"It happens at least once a week," replied Emily. "There is another Emily Silver in town who runs the Pooch Pit dog grooming service. I'm sure that she gets calls for me, too."

As they emerged onto the sidewalk in front of the Millstone Grill Restaurant they ran into Richard Fry, of McLain & Fry.

"Richard, you seem distressed," said Arthur.

"Distressed is putting it mildly," replied Richard. "We have had a terrible disaster at the office. I spent the morning doing damage control. I'm sure we are going to lose a big client."

"What happened?" asked Emily.

"Our client thought his wife was cheating on him. He asked us to investigate. We had our investigator follow her around and check on whom she was seeing – all the usual stuff. It turned out that there was nothing to it. The wife was clean. So we wrap up the case and send the client the bill. Unfortunately, instead of using his office address, which my secretary updated on my Rolodex, the bill went to his home address because someone forgot to update his address in the billing system. His wife opened it up and read it. Now she wants to divorce him and he wants to sue us for malpractice for disclosing confidential information."

"No good deed goes unpunished," said Emily.

"Sounds like you need better law practice software," offered Arthur. He pulled open the heavy door of the Millstone Grill and they entered. The air inside smelled of roast chicken and baked bread. Arthur suddenly felt very hungry.

"So how do you avoid those screw-ups?" asked Richard.

"If you're still using separate systems like a Rolodex, and billing system, and a file contact sheet," continued Arthur, "you're not only double- or triple-entering the same information, just forget to update that information in one place and you're guaranteed to mess up by using the wrong information at some time in the future."

"So what's the solution?" asked Richard.

"It's really very easy," explained Arthur. "You simply have just one correct mailing address for each person, in one place – your integrated practice management system. Whenever you generate bill, draft a letter or include the client's mailing address on any form or document, it's always pulled and inserted from the one correct source. No more double- or triple-entry, no more searching for the address on the last document you sent, or looking it up in the case file and retyping it.

"Clients move, get divorced, and change jobs. Older clients die and leave behind widows or widowers. Contact information must be constantly updated, and with the appropriate software a change can be made in one place and be used everywhere."

The Rotary president approached Arthur. "I read today that Arthur Simon was named to the board of the art museum. Sounds like good news – that will be a dollar, Arthur."

Arthur laughed. "I think they meant some other Arthur Simon."

"Nope, the article showed your photo. Definitely you. Pay up!"

Arthur dropped five dollars into the basket. "Okay, it was me. It's all for a good cause!"

☑ Simon says: Avoid double-entry, embarrassing mix-ups and potential malpractice by making sure that the correct contact information is always pulled from your single central contacts database.

19: The Brand Myth

To build a big brand you have to act like a big firm

"Do you think I can get her autograph?" It was a Sunday afternoon and Georgia Billings was in line at the bookstore, where Tammy Williams, the legendary country singer, was signing copies of her new memoir.

"Absolutely," replied Arthur Simon. "Tammy is known for her personal dedication to her fans. She will stay here until she has personally greeted every single man, woman, grandpa, grandma, and child. That's one reason why she is so successful."

"I'm glad we have a different approach in the legal business," said Georgia.

"How so?"

"At Scott & Billings we have a policy that Dick and I do not pick up the phone ourselves. We leave that to Angie and the other legal assistants. We believe that it gives us the big important firm image. You know, like Axel, Gunz & Rose. When you call them you get a receptionist. You never get Mr. Big Gunz."

The line inched forward. At the table Arthur could see Tammy Williams with her trademark beehive hairdo and red lipstick, smiling and signing books.

"Is your firm as big as Axel, Gunz & Rose?" asked Arthur.

Georgia laughed. "Of course not – you know that! They have a thousand people working for them."

"I knew Big Gunz when he was your age. He worked at a firm just like Scott & Billings. And do you know something? He busted his rear end for his clients. He used to give his clients a business card with his direct number. He would say, 'Call me anytime.' He always answered his own phone. I know, because I hired him to handle a case for me and he was always available. He made me feel like I was his only client."

"But that's not the way it is anymore at Axel, Gunz & Rose. They have an aura of power."

"I'll bet that Gunz still answers plenty of his own phone calls. His clients are paying huge fees. They demand and they get personal access."

Suddenly Arthur and Georgia were joined by Odell Cochran. "Are you here to see Tammy Williams too?" asked Arthur.

"No, I just happened to pop in for a newspaper."

"You have a new television ad, don't you?"

"Odell smiled. "You bet, and it's really paying off!"

"How so?" asked Georgia.

"Last year we commissioned a series of television ads designed to boost our personal injury business. The ads were created by a high-powered ad agency and featured scenes of car wrecks and testimony by satisfied clients. At the end of the ad was the firm's phone number.

"The ad was visually powerful but the response was disappointing. We didn't even recoup the cost of production and broadcast. So then I listened to a marketing genius who had a different approach. We hired a small production company and brought a camera to my office. I sat on the edge of my desk and spoke directly to the camera the way I would speak to a client. I told the unseen audience that I would provide a high level of personal service and that every case was important and that I and the entire firm was committed to making every effort to get a favorable outcome in every case. I invited the viewer to call for a free consultation to see if we could take the case.

"The new ad went on the air and the response was immediate. Inquiries from prospects doubled in two weeks. When people called the firm they invariably asked for me by name because I had made a personal connection."

Arthur, Georgia and Odell found themselves standing in front of Tammy Williams, radiant in a rhinestone-studded jacket and matching skirt. With her perfect hair and makeup the singer looked as if she had just arrived from the farm instead of having been sitting at the table signing autographs for the past three hours.

Georgia presented her book to be signed. "How on earth do you do this all day?" she asked. "Don't you get tired?"

Tammy flashed her big smile. "Honey," she said, "If folks are willing to stand in line to see me, then I reckon I can sit here long enough to meet them. After all, there's no substitute for the real Tammy Williams."

"And," added Arthur, "There's no substitute for the real Georgia Billings."

☑ Simon says: The best 'brand' is you. Build it one satisfied client at a time. Keep it real, make it personal. If you can make every client feel as though they are the only one that matters you'll be a true superstar.

20: The Advertising Myth

There's no such thing as "too successful" when it comes to advertising

The day was hot and the state fair was crowded with tourists and farmers and families with cranky children. Arthur Simon and Larry Kohn were strolling past the pens of blue-ribbon Guernsey cows, trying to avoid getting run over by the soccer moms with the giant baby strollers.

"Let's get something cool to drink," said Arthur. They made their way through the crowd to the refreshment stand. "Look Larry, they have that new Atomic Cola. It's being advertised like crazy on television; a huge marketing campaign, with tie-ins and sponsorships and direct mail. The beverage company is spending millions to launch the product."

"I suppose we should try it," replied Larry. They ordered two bottles. After a moment they looked at each other.

"Are you thinking what I'm thinking?"

"This stuff tastes like crap."

"I agree. It's got that weird chemical taste from the artificial sweetener. Yecch."

They discreetly tossed the bottles in the recycling bin.

"Hey, look, it's Rodney Strong from Strong & Silver," said Arthur. "Rodney, what brings you to the state fair? You look like you're on top of the world."

"Hi Arthur. Hi Larry. Nice to see you both," said Rodney "I'm here to meet a client who is showing his prize stallion. But I'm excited because our firm is rolling out a new advertising campaign this week. We've got a redesigned website, new television ads, and a new print ad campaign. It's going to put the name Strong & Silver everywhere!"

"That's wonderful," said Larry. "Are you sure you can handle the business?"

"Of course. Gee, Larry, I thought you'd approve. After all, you're the legal rainmaker guru."

Larry spied a vacant picnic table under a shady tree. "Let's sit for a moment." They sat on the rustic benches.

"There are two results of a big advertising campaign that many firms have unfortunately learned the hard way. One is that their advertising is not successful, the other is they are too successful.

"In the advertising business there's an old saying," continued Larry. "It goes like this: there is no quicker way to kill a bad product than with good advertising."

"Too successful? How's that possible?" asked Rodney.

"Have you heard of Atomic Cola?"

"Of course! Who hasn't? It's the new soft drink sensation. You can't turn on the TV or go on the Internet without seeing their advertisements."

"Have you tried it?"

"Yes. My daughter bought some at the supermarket. I thought it tasted vile."

Arthur chimed in, "Check this out." He handed Rodney his PDA with the latest news headlines displayed.

Rodney read the story out loud. "The Acme Beverage Company today announced that due to poor customer response it is suspending the product launch of Atomic Cola."

"It is a new product disaster," said Arthur. "The death of Atomic Cola was hastened by the very successful advertising campaign. Because of the saturation advertising everybody tried it, and unfortunately the product didn't meet the promises."

"What has that got to do with advertising our firm?" asked Rodney.

"Either your advertising won't be successful, in which case it will just cost you some money, or it's extremely successful and new clients come streaming through the doors. Now that's when you have real problems. Ask yourself, 'Do I have the systems and people in place to handle the surge? Are we capable of meeting the promises of our advertising and the expectations of all our clients? Will things slip through the cracks?'"

"This makes a lot of sense," agreed Rodney. "Now if you'll excuse me, I'm going to get back to the office. I have some planning to do."

☑ Simon says: The fastest way to ruin your reputation is with advertising that's too successful. Make sure your systems and staff are ready to handle the surge. Ramp it up, advertise judiciously.

21: The Document Assembly Myth
Document assembly software isn't worth the effort

The University Club was quiet on this Tuesday evening. In the luxurious oak-paneled lounge, under the stuffed moose head hanging on the wall, Dick Scott sat at a table, alone. Before him was a double shot of whiskey.

When Arthur entered the lounge he intended only to have a quick martini before heading to the main dining room to join a group for dinner. When he saw Dick he waved a greeting, but the young lawyer's glum demeanor prompted Arthur to carry his martini over to the table.

"You must be meeting someone," offered Arthur.

"Yeah. Jack Daniels. And then his pals Old Grand Dad and Jim Beam. "

"That sounds a bit grim." Arthur pulled up one of the big leather club chairs.

"I just wanted to visit the club one last time before I get sued for malpractice and disbarred and have to go flip burgers for a living," said Dick.

"Tell me about it."

"We got hired by Greenbacks Incorporated to handle a big real estate deal. Angie, Georgia and I put together the documents. We started with a copy of the ones we'd used for another big client and just changed the names. You know, cut and paste. All very standard, we do it all the time. We sent the package over to them to sign. Everything was fine until they noticed references to the other client's transaction that we missed cutting and pasting and inadvertently revealed some things we should have kept confidential. Plus, we overlooked a critical date. If they had signed what we prepared they would have been liable for performance that they couldn't meet. They would have been screwed. Instead, we're screwed."

Arthur had an ace up his sleeve, but he wanted to wait before revealing it to Dick. Instead he said, "Why are you still assembling documents by hand? Handcrafting is fine for expensive whiskey, but as you see, with the risks of missing things, it could be way too costly for a law firm."

"We looked into document assembly," said Dick, "but since every client is unique and every document has to be customized anyway, I didn't think it made sense to spend the time and money to set it up, learn how to use it, and then convert our master documents into templates."

Arthur asked Dick, "Do you think it's better to set up a document template once that will automatically fill some of the blanks with the data you already have on the client and matter, or would you rather have to search for a recent version to start with, save it to a new name, and begin cutting and pasting endlessly, and hope you don't miss something and inadvertently reveal confidential information?"

"Put that way, there's really no choice, is there," said Dick. "Now all I need is a Wayback Machine like Mr. Peabody had on *The Rocky and Bullwinkle Show*. I could go back in time and instead of being a chump I could be a hero, and Greenbacks wouldn't be suing me."

"Well, perhaps that won't happen."

"How?"

It was time for Arthur to reveal that ace up his sleeve. "I went to law school with Dave Greenbacks. He was a tough kid from the projects, but we got along famously. I even dated his sister Maria for a while. We still see each other, mostly at the theatre. I'll give him a call and ask him to cut you a break. He was once young, too, and he'll understand what it's like to make a stupid mistake."

"Thanks, Arthur," said Dick. "I guess I owe you one."

"Just maintain your friendships. Perhaps some day you'll be able to help out a kid who needs a break too."

☑ Simon says: Don't risk delivering documents with "leftovers" from prior clients. Document assembly combines your practice management data with your word processor template to produce better documents while protecting your firm from potential malpractice.

22: The Office Visit Myth
Worthwhile prospects will come to your office

When Arthur Simon stopped by Dick's office at lunchtime, Dick was busy opening a big carton.

"Looks like a delivery from that online bookstore," said Arthur.

"Yes, it is," replied Dick. "I ordered a couple of James Bond novels, a book on sea shells, and a book about old houses that I'm going to give to my mother for her birthday."

"It certainly is convenient to buy books online," said Arthur.

"They have an amazing system," said Dick as he arranged the books on his desk. "When you log on to the website they automatically bring up your personalized account. They give you suggestions about titles that are related to the ones that you have bought in the past. When something new is published that fits your profile they send you an email. All of my personal information is saved, so using the shopping basket checkout system is very easy. They practically do everything for you."

"And you happily pay the bill," said Arthur.

Dick laughed. "Well, I suppose that I sometimes get carried away. It's just so effortless."

"Personally, I still shop at my corner bookstore – the proprietor does everything your online store does. But to each his own. Ready for lunch? We're going to be joined by an old friend of mine."

A few minutes later they sat down at a corner table at Chez Panini. "Dick, I'd like you to meet my colleague Brian Whitaker. He's a good man to know."

"Nice to meet you, Brian," said Dick. "I hope you don't mind if I cry on Arthur's shoulder."

"Why, what's the matter?" said Arthur.

"I think maybe I have cooties."

"Cooties?" said Brian. "I haven't heard that expression since my days at Roosevelt Elementary School."

"I don't know how else to describe it," said Dick. "But it's a serious problem. In the past two weeks I've been stood up by three prospects. These are people who contacted me with significant legal problems. I talked to each one on the phone and in each case we set up an appointment for the following day. But none of them showed up. Three times I sat there in my office, waiting like a dummy, with our conference room booked and my partner giving me dirty looks. Like I said, I feel like I have cooties."

The waiter arrived and they placed their orders: *pasta Marinara, pollo al gorgonzola,* and *tortellini al forno,* with *insalata Caprese* to start.

"Brian, I'm sure Dick would benefit from your accumulated wisdom," said Arthur as he sampled a ripe *Roma* tomato.

"My pleasure," said Brian with a smile. "Dick, I can assure you that every lawyer has been stood up by a prospect. But perhaps you are making a mistake in the process. Tell me how you handle setting up the initial consultation. I assume it is free of charge?"

"Yes," replied Dick. "On the phone I briefly review their problem, and if it's a case that I think I can handle then I invite them to come to the office for a consultation. So that our meeting can be more productive I tell the prospect what documents they should gather and bring to the meeting."

"And the prospect agrees to this?"

"Yes."

"And you never hear from them again."

"Yes."

Brian took a piece of *ciabatta* bread and dipped it in olive oil. "My young friend, you stand accused and convicted of scaring away your clients."

"Scaring them? I thought I was helping them."

"Yes, but you made a very common mistake. When someone is seeking legal representation they do not want to make a commitment until they feel confident and secure. By asking the prospect to gather documents, you present conditions that the prospect feels compelled to fulfill. You put an obstacle in front of them. You skip an important step – the get-to-know-you step."

"What should I do?" asked Dick.

"Be very accommodating," replied Brian. "Make it easy. If the prospect asks about bringing documents, just say that whatever they want to bring is fine. No pressure. Of course you need to project an air of professionalism. No one will hire a lawyer who sits around shooting the breeze while the clock ticks. I am sure that being professional is no problem for you, but you need to open the door and let them walk through it."

Dick snapped his fingers. "I get it! Just like the online bookstore. Take down the barriers. Make it so easy and so effortless that the process becomes invisible."

"That's right," said Arthur. "Ah, here comes our lunch. *Buon appetito!*"

☑ Simon says: Don't scare away prospects by giving them assignments before your initial consultation. Make it as easy to do business with you as shopping online.

23: The Competition Myth

You only compete against other lawyers

Arthur Simon and Brian Whitaker met Dick Scott on the steps of the Museum of Natural History. "Are you here for the same reason we are?" asked Arthur.

"You bet, to see the new Tyrannosaurus Rex skeleton!" replied Dick.

"My colleague Brian Whitaker and I were discussing untraditional ways of running a law practice that might interest you," replied Arthur. "But I see that we need to buy our tickets. Let's return to our discussion after we see the exhibit."

They entered the museum, and in a few moments were standing in front of the massive dinosaur.

"T Rex was a fearsome predator," remarked Arthur. "For more than 150 million years, dinosaurs ruled the Earth. We humans have been here less than one percent of that time. And this guy was at the top of the food chain."

"It's amazing that they reigned supreme for so long. Do you think they knew when their time was up?" asked Dick.

"My young friend, the mighty T Rex succumbed to something against which it and other dinosaurs had no defense. Scientists call it the Cretaceous-Tertiary extinction event, and it occurred approximately 65.5 million years ago. It was a large-scale mass extinction of animal and plant species in a geologically short period of time – anywhere from a few years to a few thousand years. Relative to the age of the Earth, which is 4.5 billion years, it happened in the blink of an eye."

"They never knew what hit them," mused Dick. "I'm glad that in the legal business there's no chance of getting blindsided like this guy did. We know who we're competing against."

"And who would that be?" asked Brian.

"Other lawyers, of course."

"With that kind of attitude you will end up as extinct as the Tyrannosaurus Rex. Or the Dodo bird," mused Arthur.

"How so?"

"Go ahead, Brian. Enlighten my young friend here."

"Dick," began Brian, "the legal marketplace has changed. Now people can get legal help from non-lawyer sources. They can go on the Internet and download self help legal guides. They can go to websites that will prepare legal forms for them like wills, trusts, corporations, and trademarks. They can go to paralegal services and get divorce forms. They can even get check-the-box forms from the courts and use court staff to help them fill out and file the forms. They can go to small claims court without an attorney. They can even have their case settled on television by Judge Judy."

"I don't know. I think there will always be lawyers," replied Dick.

"That may be, but you need to step back and see how the legal landscape is changing," said Brian. "On May 21, 2007, in the case of *Winkelman v. Parma City School District*, the Supreme Court of the United States ruled in favor of Ohio parents who sued a school district over their child's special education needs under the Individuals with Disabilities Education Act (IDEA). The Winkelmans had filed suit without using a lawyer. The case generated interest after the Cleveland Bar Association launched an investigation of the Winkelmans and other Ohio parents for the Unauthorized Practice of Law.

"The Supreme Court held that parents do not need to be represented by a lawyer. Instead parents have independent, enforceable rights under IDEA and that they may represent themselves in court to vindicate those rights. The couple, Sandee and Jeff Winkelman, are not lawyers, and had argued they could not afford a lawyer and had the best understanding of their child's special needs."

Dick whistled softly. "I looks like lawyers don't have a monopoly on the law anymore. So how do we adapt?"

"More and more lawyers are offering non-traditional service and fee arrangements," explained Brian, "such as unbundled services where we limit the scope of our work and liability. For example, we might just handle the document preparation for the client to use in pro per. In conjunction with the Internet and email, we're even seeing firms owned by lawyers but not offering representation charging flat fees for a set menu of services and offering money back guarantees. Instead of clients they have customers that they never even see face to face."

"Wow, those sound like serious threats to the old dinosaur firms," said Dick.

"We live in exciting times, my friend," said Arthur. "It's up to you to see and seize the opportunities."

☑ Simon says: Don't be a dinosaur when it comes to services you offer and how you deliver and bill for them. With the Internet, your competition is no longer limited to just local practitioners. There are T Rex-sized opportunities for those who think outside the box.

24: The Hands-On Myth

Great lawyers are always working in their practices

"Tell me again why we are visiting the Topsfield Fair," said Georgia Billings to Arthur Simon as they strolled past the carnival attractions and cotton-candy stands.

"Because you need a break and I want to see the award-winning roses," replied Arthur.

"But I have so much work to do! I cannot afford to wander around these fairgrounds when I know that messages are piling up back at the office. Aren't you the one who is always preaching instant communication, and how we should always be ready to talk to a client, and that even a few minutes' delay can mean the difference between getting a client and missing the opportunity?"

"Yes, I say all of those things. But tell me – isn't Dick back at the office covering for you?"

"Yes."

"That's effective teamwork, and one reason why you have chosen not to have a solo practice. When a client or prospect calls the office, Dick is perfectly qualified to provide excellent customer service. Ah, here we are. One of my favorite attractions."

They stopped in front of the Ferris wheel. "A magnificent invention!" said Arthur as they bought two tickets. "Originally designed by George Washington Gale Ferris, Jr., as a landmark for the 1893 World's Columbian Exposition in Chicago, his wheel could carry over two thousand people at one time. Ferris wanted to build something to rival the Eiffel Tower, which had been built four years earlier for the Paris Exposition. This version is of course much smaller than the original, but well worth the experience."

The wheel stopped and Georgia and Arthur stepped into the small circular compartment. The tattooed attendant closed the safety door and the Ferris wheel lurched into motion. Georgia and Arthur were borne aloft, and seconds later they were enjoying the breathtaking view of the fairgrounds, the surrounding parking lots, and in the distance the blue rolling hills that faded to the pale horizon.

"To me, the Ferris wheel is a perfect metaphor for life and work," said Arthur.

"How so?" said Georgia as they swung back down towards the ground.

"When we are close to the ground, as we are now, we see everything in detail. The people standing in line, the babies in strollers, the guy eating a foot-long hot dog. They are all very near to us and we see them very clearly. But what we cannot see is the overall view, the big picture. We are too close."

The Ferris wheel lofted them skyward again. "But now we leave the close-up picture behind and we are taken up to where we can see into the distance. The people below us become less individual, but in return we see where we are. Look, over there, is the highway interchange. Over the hills beyond you can just see the city skyline. In the other direction you can see the blue ridge of the mountain range. Spectacular, isn't it?"

"Yes," replied Georgia. "It's interesting to see the layout of the fairground –I had no idea that the building where they have the art show is just a few steps away from the entrance. The way they route you down the midway with all the carnival games, it seems like it's a long way to get there. But when you are up here you can see all the shortcuts."

"And when the Ferris wheel brings you back down to earth you lose the perspective and are plunged once again into a world of details," said Arthur.

"I see what you mean," said Georgia. "But something about taking time off, not working on client matters, seems lazy."

"Nothing could be further from the truth! The wise lumber jack knows he'll get a lot more wood chopped when he regularly stops to sharpen his axe."

☑ Simon says: If you're spending all of your time working *in* your practice, when will you have time to work *on* your practice? Make it a priority. Block a weekly time slot on your schedule and work on your office systems and procedures, meet with advisors, and step back from the practice to see it from outside the box.

25: The Legalese Myth
Using legal terminology commands respect

"Have you ever heard of a mondegreen?" asked Arthur Simon as he flipped through a paperback book while waiting at the train station.

"A what?" replied Jackson Green, the probate lawyer, who was sitting on a bench with his briefcase at his side and a Styrofoam cup of coffee in his hand.

"Mondegreen. The word was coined by the Scottish writer Sylvia Wright in a 1954 article in *Harper's Magazine*. It means a misunderstood song lyric or phrase, usually with humorous results. For example, the line 'Excuse me while I kiss the sky' from the Jimi Hendrix song 'Purple Haze' is commonly misunderstood as 'Excuse me while I kiss this guy.'"

"I thought that's what it was – 'kiss this guy.'"

"No. Here's another classic mondegreen: in the Pledge of Allegiance most schoolchildren think the word 'indivisible' is 'invisible' – you know, 'one nation, under God, invisible'. When I was a kid I was sure it meant God was invisible."

At that moment Charlie Hawley flopped down on the bench next to Arthur. "I'm sure glad this horrible day is over!" he announced to no one in particular.

Arthur took the cue and closed his book. "Tough day, Charlie?"

"Here's what happened. I have a client who owns a construction company that builds highways and bridges. His cousin runs the company. My guy gets busted for money laundering and racketeering. The feds want to put him away for twenty years. On a conference call I tell him that we need his cousin's deposition. His cousin was in the hospital with cancer. Nothing happens and my client never gets back to me. The hearing date is approaching and I ask my client again to connect me with the cousin for his deposition because we need it for the hearing. He says the cousin has passed away and he doesn't know anything about his cousin's deep position.

"I say, 'Deep position? What are you talking about?'

"My client says, 'I don't know, you're the one that asked me about my cousin's deep position. I know for sure he wasn't a snitch, so I thought it didn't matter.' Now we're screwed because the cousin's testimony was critical."

"So now your position is deep doo-doo," said Jackson.

"Very funny," groaned Charlie.

"Once I had a client who was the victim of copyright infringement," said Arthur. "I told my client that I was sending the defendant a letter *in terrorem*. My client responded that the defendant did not live in Terrorem but in Milwaukee."

"I had a guy who was accused of shredding his mother's will, from which he had been cut out," said Jackson. "I told my client that a key issue was *mens rea*. My client chided me and said it was his mother's will, not his father's, so it's women's rea, not *mens rea*."

"How about this one," said Arthur. "I had a client tell me that he wanted to sue his stepchild's school board, and he knew he had a right to sue because he had 'low custody.' I had no idea what 'low custody' was until I figured out that somewhere he had heard the expression *'locus standi.'*"

"Okay!" said Charlie. "I get the point. From now on I will speak to my clients in plain English."

☑ Simon says: Latin phrases from centuries ago don't belong in this century. The more plainly you speak and write, the more your audience will understand and appreciate you.

26: The Court Rules Myth

Keep court rules handy to know what's next

At the Curtain Call Pub, Arthur Simon and Jane Smith were enjoying dinner after an evening at the theatre. "*Romeo and Juliet* is one of my favorite plays," said Jane. "But I always feel so sad after seeing it, and tonight is no exception. To think – if the messenger sent by Friar Laurence had reached Romeo in time, Romeo would have known that Juliet wasn't dead but just in a trance from the potion and they both might have lived!"

"Indeed," said Arthur as he dipped a shrimp in cocktail sauce, "It is tragic that so much can depend upon a few minutes' delay."

At that moment their colleague Emily Silver entered the restaurant and, seeing the two, joined them at their table.

"What's the matter, Emily? You look upset," said Arthur.

"This has been a terrible day," replied Emily. "I'm sure that we are going to be sued for malpractice."

"Here, have a glass of wine. Tell us what happened," said Jane.

"We have a client who filed suit against his business partners because he wanted to quit the partnership. We couldn't work out a deal with the remaining partners so we went to court. A judgment was handed down and we thought the case was closed. A week later our client called and requested an appeal. We agreed; then my partner Rodney went on vacation and things got busy. I thought Rodney had gotten an extension from the court, and it wasn't until sixty-two days later that I filed the appeal."

"Two days too late," said Arthur.

"So said the court. I guess we just got confused about the timing. Now we're screwed and our client may sue us."

"Have some shrimp cocktail," said Arthur, "I can't go back in time and fix the problem, but I can help you avoid making the same mistake again."

"How can you do that?" inquired Emily.

"With software that knows and automates deadlines based on court rules, you can simply select the rule and the software will automatically calculate all the deadlines for you and enter them on your calendar. In this case, the trial rule could have calendared the deadline for appeal, as well as reminders that could appear on both the responsible attorney's calendar as well as his or her secretary's."

"How does it know the rules in my jurisdiction?" asked Emily.

"The software vendor keeps the rules updated for many jurisdictions. If you're out in Timbuktu, you may have to start with a similar rule and adjust it, but then it's easy to keep it updated if you're practicing there."

"So no more counting days on the wall calendar or my fingers – the software does all that for me?"

"Even better, it calculates all of the related deadlines, not just your next step. You simply calendar the trigger event and all related events are scheduled automatically. When you reschedule any event, all the related dates change according to the rule. For example, when you calendar a trial, all related discovery cutoffs, witness designations and other dates are automatically calendared. Move the trial date, the deadlines are recalculated."

"It may be too late for Romeo and Juliet, but it's not for me," said Emily. "Tomorrow morning I'm going to get set up so we never miss a court deadline again. How about another order of shrimp cocktail?"

☑ Simon says: To be more than one step ahead and reduce your risk of costly deadline mistakes, use software that automatically calendars deadlines based on local court rules.

27: The Superstar Myth

Paralegals are interchangeable; the real value comes from you

At the University Club Arthur Simon was entering the dining room when he met his colleague Oscar McLain, the sports and entertainment lawyer.

"Arthur, I'd like you to meet an up-and-coming young lawyer," said Oscar. "Randy Max, meet Arthur Simon." They shook hands. "Would you join us for dinner?" said Oscar.

"I'd be delighted," said Arthur.

They ordered the daily specials: cream of mushroom soup and a house salad with raspberry vinaigrette dressing, followed by prime rib.

As Arthur poured wine he noticed that Randy Max seemed to be fairly bursting with pride. "So, how's it going?" offered Arthur to start the conversation. "Oscar told me that you are in criminal defense."

"I thought you would have seen me on television," replied Randy.

Arthur chose to overlook this rather vain response. "I don't watch much TV, thanks. Were you on a big case?"

"As big as they get. I defended a sailor who kept a pet orangutan. The primate escaped from its pen and brutally murdered a woman and her daughter in their apartment. The orangutan stuffed the daughter's body up the chimney. It was a sensational trial, and the sailor was accused of murder. I got him off."

"Congratulations," said Arthur. "To what do you attribute your victory?"

"My courtroom presentation, of course," replied Randy. "I had the jury in the palm of my hand. They were with me from my opening to the closing. The DA never had a chance."

"Well, it looks like you're off to a good start," said Arthur. "What's next? How do you plan on building your practice?"

Randy laughed. "I'm not worried. Randy Max is a household name. I'm sure that I will be getting all the clients I can possibly handle."

"I hope so," replied Arthur.

A month later Arthur saw Randy at the bar association annual meeting. The young superstar seemed downcast, so Arthur made it a point to sit next to him. "You seem rather quiet," Arthur said.

"I'm in big trouble," Randy replied.

"After the big orangutan murder case I thought you were on top of the world."

"That's what I thought, too. I've got another big case right now – the body of a young woman was found in the river, and her fiancée was arrested. It's a complex case with lots of forensics and expert witnesses. We were building a solid defense until two of my legal assistants gave me their notice."

"They're quitting? Why?"

"They say I don't pay them enough. What do I know? They're just paralegals. But they did all the grunt work. I've got a hearing in a week and I don't know a damn thing about this case. I'm screwed."

"Did these two work on the orangutan case?"

"Sure. They got all the stuff together for me to take to court."

Arthur took his young colleague by the arm. "When I first met you I didn't want to say anything to you, but now I feel a professional obligation. Your paralegals are not just anonymous drones. They are the backbone of your practice. The average salary for a paralegal in our town with one year of experience is $36,000. With five years experience it's $50,000. The annual salary for top paralegals can be over $80,000 a year. Were you paying in that range?"

Randy's eyes widened. "No, not at all."

"It's no wonder they jumped ship at the first opportunity. At a dozen other law firms in town they could get paid what they are worth. My advice to you is to contact them today and beg them to come back by offering a competitive salary."

"Okay, I'll do that."

"And one more thing. If you want to build a reputation as a winning attorney, you need to remember that you are part of a team. You may be the quarterback, but without ten other tough players on your side you're just an empty suit."

A few months later Arthur was pleased to read in the paper that Randy Max had gotten an acquittal for his client – and in the article Randy thanked his dedicated and tireless paralegals.

☑ Simon says: Superstars know it's what's behind the scene that counts. Give your staff the technology and training to be superstars at their jobs, and they'll give you what you need to be a superstar at yours.

28: The Free Advice Myth

Websites don't attract good clients, just people seeking free advice

On a beautiful Sunday afternoon Arthur Simon and Gunter Enz decided to do a little road rally in the back country. Arthur took out his vintage 1968 Corvette convertible. Gunter took his new Porsche Boxter S. They headed out to visit Arthur's colleague Fred Glassman, who had a solo practice.

When they pulled into the driveway of the rambling farmhouse Fred was in his beekeeper's outfit, tending the beehives. After a few minutes Fred took off the hat and gloves and greeted them.

"That's a beautiful Stingray," remarked Fred. "The first year of the Mako Shark design, if I'm not mistaken."

"Thanks," replied Arthur. "Technically, it's not called a Stingray. During the 1968 model year the name 'Stingray' doesn't appear anywhere on the car."

Fred examined the gleaming Corvette. "Darned if you aren't correct as usual, my friend."

"Fred, meet my friend and racing buddy Gunter Enz. He's a pretty good driver and an expert on marketing law practices using the Internet."

"Nice to meet you, Gunter."

"How are the bees?" asked Gunter.

"They're terrific this year," replied Fred. "I just planted a patch of lavender by the fence that they seem to love. We're going to get a nice batch of honey. But I may have to sell the hives."

"Why?"

"Business is down. It's really terrible. Must be the economy. I have to spend more time at the office just to make ends meet. I can't devote the necessary time to the bees."

They went inside for lemonade made with fresh honey and then sat on the big front porch.

"I happened to be online yesterday and I saw your website," said Gunter.

Fred shrugged. "My legal assistant made me put up the website. She says everyone's doing it. I think it's a big waste of

time. Everybody knows that people who go online to find law
are just trolling for free information."

"The Internet is in every home, office, library, and cell phone,"
replied Gunter. "Your legal assistant is steering you in the right
direction. She knows that today virtually everyone has access to
the Internet. Your website is your electronic shingle, hanging
outside your door for all the world to see."

Fred sipped his lemonade. "Do you really think that people
look for an attorney on line?"

"Absolutely, good clients are searching online for just the right
attorney. Surveys show that prospects view an average of 4.8
websites before they select a lawyer. Your website is your chance
to convince them to contact you and start a dialogue."

"But all they want is free information."

"Yes. That's the whole point. The Internet is all about free
information, from Wikipedia to Google to the website of Fred
Glassman, Esq. People have become conditioned to going online
to learn about what's happening in the world. Free information is
a funnel that leads to paying clients. Your competitors know this.
That's why every one of them has a website. And every prospect
is comparing them with you based on your website, and you don't
even know it."

"I didn't see that, but I do now," groaned Fred. "But a website is
a big investment."

"How much did you invest in your lavender?" asked Gunter.
"When you add up all the time, labor, and materials, even without
the value of the real estate you've devoted to it, I'm sure it's quite
a bit. But you don't mind, do you?"

"Of course not!" responded Fred. "How else am I going to get
my bees to make honey unless I provide them with pollen? By the
time I sell the honey I've made a nice profit."

"So you attract the bees with lavender that gives them plenty
of pollen to make honey. Doesn't it make sense to attract
prospects with your website and give them plenty of content so
they'll make an appointment with you?"

"Well now that you put it that way, I suppose so. What do I
need to have on my website?" asked Fred.

ebsite one that attracts the most prospects
most new clients for you, you'll want to give
of your work, provide answers to questions your
king, and give them a reason to contact you now.
rospect so that they feel as though they can make
an in... choice. They don't want to feel stupid when they
talk to you. validate your professional image as an authority on
their problems. Encourage them to contact you and initiate a
consultation."

Fred looked worried. "I don't know," he said. "I feel
uncomfortable about putting too much legal information on my
website."

"Why?" chimed in Arthur. "The law is the same for everyone.
Lawyers aren't like soft drink companies or technology firms. We
don't have trade secrets. Sure, some people will try to handle
their cases themselves. But when the chips are down, they will
want a qualified lawyer."

Fred snapped his fingers. "Of course!" he exclaimed. "I got a
call the other day from a woman who sounded like she had read
one of those how-to books on lawyering. I'm afraid I was a bit
short with her. I didn't realize that she probably had been to a
bunch of websites and had read their content."

"She was at step three, but you blew it," said Gunter. "You
thought she was just trying to pick your brain."

A honeybee landed on Fred's arm. He looked at it for a
moment. "Get back to work," he said. "I'm not giving you free
pollen for nothing!" The bee flew off towards the lavender plants.

"Okay," said Fred. "From now on I'll tend to my website with
the same care and energy that I give to my garden."

☑ Simon says: Your website content is the pollen that attracts
honeybees. Over 90% of those looking for legal help on the Internet will
become someone's client.

29: The Smoking Gun Myth

With gigabytes of data, it's almost impossible to find the smoking gun

At the University Club's Thursday night poker game Charlie Hawley of Pinto & Hawley was considering his hand. The pot had grown to three figures and there was excitement in the room as one by one the players folded. On the third betting round Charlie folded. After the showdown he dejectedly rose from his seat and joined Arthur Simon and Albert Barsocchini at their table in the lounge.

"No more poker for me. What a lousy hand I had!" he said.

"What did you have?" asked Albert.

"The worst possible cards. A Queen, ten, deuce, and ace. The guy who won the pot had four of a kind."

"Weren't you playing hi-lo?" asked Arthur.

"I'm not sure," replied Charlie. "It was a game called Omaha. Yes, I suppose I heard something about hi-lo."

"You need to be more attentive," said Arthur. "The five communal flop cards included a three, four, and five. You could have made five-high straight for the best low hand at the table."

"A what?"

"A straight from ace to five. Also called a 'wheel.'"

"So what?"

"In hi-lo, the pot is split between the best high hand and the best low hand. You walked away from a jackpot, my friend."

Charlie groaned. "I didn't know those were the rules."

"In Omaha, determining the best hand can be difficult. Not knowing the rules can lead to serious mistakes. Let me order you a drink."

At that moment they were joined by Fred Glassman. "Whatever this young fellow is having, make mine a double," he groused. "What an awful day I've had."

"I thought you had a big day in court," offered Albert.

"I got blindsided!" replied Fred. "I'm defending an eco-terrorist who is accused of conspiring to blow up a bulldozer. We gave the assistant district attorney my client's emails and electronic documents, and they were clean. I thought we were in the clear because there was no evidence other than testimony from a convicted bank robber who was obviously coerced by the ADA. An easy dismissal. But the court gave the ADA a warrant to search everything: my client's computer, Facebook pages, instant messaging, his PDA, and his MySpace pages. They copied his hard drives, downloaded everything, and used technology that I've never even heard of."

"And they found something," said Albert.

"Yes. Enough to make my guy look like Timothy McVeigh. So now the ADA is saying that I was trying to hide evidence and it's too late for a deal. Instead of entering into a nice quiet plea bargain, he looking to get sanctions against me, file an ethics complaint with the state bar, and wants to make an example of my guy at a big public show trial. This is going to be horrible."

The waiter arrived with drinks. "Here's to a better tomorrow," said Albert. "In the meantime, what happened to Fred can be a lesson for us all. We need to stay informed of new boundaries in evidentiary rules. As we know, Federal Rules of Evidence Article X Rule 1001 says that 'writings' and 'recordings' consist of letters, words, or numbers, or their equivalent, set down by handwriting, typewriting, printing, photostatting, photographing, magnetic impulse, mechanical or electronic recording, or other form of data compilation. We are seeing that the word 'electronic' is getting bigger and more inclusive every day."

"Law enforcement is increasingly using social networking sites as sources of evidence," added Arthur.

"You're absolutely correct," agreed Albert. "Three cases come to mind. Police detectives in Tacoma, Washington used MySpace to prove a motive in a triple homicide case. They discovered that at least two of the victims were on one another's friends lists, and confirmed that the victims and suspects knew each other. In another case, a former elementary school teacher was sent back to prison for violating the terms of her probation. She had contacted her rape and sexual-battery victim through the MySpace blog feature. And in a murder trial the conviction turned on spyware found on the defendant's computer that he did not know he had! The forensic investigator found key logging software that had infected the computer and had logged him bragging about the killing to a friend."

"Gee Fred," said Charlie, "I'm sure glad I'm not in your shoes, my friend. Not keeping up and knowing the rules can be painful."

"Yeah, Charlie, both in poker and the law," quipped Fred.

☑ Simon says: The rules have changed. Don't risk being blindsided by discovery you should have found. New technology can find or rule out the smoking gun. Use it or risk being surprised by what your opposition finds.

30: The Separate Accounting Myth

Keep your accounting separate from your case management

"Hey Arthur, what brings you to the casino? Are you planning on wagering?"

Arthur stopped next to the one-armed bandit where Odell Cochran was busy pulling the lever and watching the screen. "Not today, Odell," replied Arthur. "I'm here with a client for the financial services convention. How are you doing?"

Odell shrugged. "Haven't won much yet. But this is a lucky machine."

"Luck? My friend, a so-called lucky machine is simply one that has the odds adjusted by the house to pay off a bit more generously than others. It helps sustain the myth."

"Myth?"

"Sure. Slot machines are programmed by the house to return a target payoff, which is usually set around 93 percent. This means that in the long run the machine will make seven cents profit for every dollar wagered. Now if a machine is set for 95 percent payoff, it will seem as though this machine is lucky, even though the house is still getting five cents per dollar wagered."

"Five cents isn't much."

"In this casino there are a thousand slot machines. If each one averages five cents profit per minute, that's over twenty-five million dollars in profit per year from slots alone!"

Odell whistled. "I wish we made that kind of money at the law firm."

"What do you mean? I heard that you were doing very well."

Odell removed his card from the slot machine and walked with Arthur over to a booth at the bar. "Sure, we're making good revenue, but our bookkeeping is a mess. I wish I had a nickel for every time we had to input a time entry, enter a payable twice – once in our payables system then in the billing system so we can get reimbursed by the client, transfer a client balance back to our accounts receivable system, fix a mistake caused by a transfer, or try to get a correct bill out to a client. We use one system for logging our time and printing out bills. We use another for accounting. We use a spreadsheet for maintaining trust accounts. When clients pay their bills we've got to

74

update all three! And even then an attorney looking at a client's case file can't tell whether the client is current or past due, or what his trust balance might be. We seldom balance the books, we miss estimated tax payments, and we never know how much cash we have in our accounts. Our accountants cost us a fortune and they never have the answers that we want."

Arthur motioned for the server and drinks were ordered. "Odell, you have an office full of brilliant lawyers. Why are you still using three different programs for case management, time and billing, and accounting?"

Odell sipped his Bermuda Rum Swizzle. "Arthur, I'm no computer genius. I can write contracts and send emails – that's about it."

"That's the beauty of the new technology, you don't have to be a techno geek to use it," replied Arthur. "Everyone in your firm can have all their clients, cases, and calendars at their fingertips, and whenever they handle a calendar event, enter a note, draft or review a document, link an email, or make a phone call, they simply click the bill button and their times are recorded. Instead of three programs, you capture time, print the bills, reconcile bank accounts, and print all your financial reports from one."

"So there's no more duplicating or transferring data from one system to another?" Odell asked incredulously.

"Now you're starting to get it," Arthur said reassuringly.

"With such a system I bet I could save a nickel on every time entry we make. That ought to pay off better than these slot machines," said Odell.

Arthur chuckled. "Jackpot!"

☑ Simon says: Stop duplicating or transferring time, billing, and accounting between programs. Use one integrated system to keep your finances in balance and make life easier on everyone – your timekeepers, your clients, and your accountants.

31: The Discovery Myth

Volunteer nothing – the more difficult you make discovery the better

After a spirited round of golf, Arthur Simon and his colleague Albert Barsocchini retired to the clubhouse for dinner. They were joined by Raymond Hamilton, a young lawyer with a specialty in corporate law.

Over a first course of vichyssoise and Waldorf salad they tested each other with trivia questions.

"Who can tell me who John Banner was?" asked Albert.

"John Banner was a Jewish Austrian-American actor," replied Arthur. "He survived a Nazi concentration camp and ironically became a household name in the 1960s when he played the role of Sergeant Schultz in the television series *Hogan's Heroes*."

"And what was his famous catch phrase?" asked Albert.

Arthur laughed at the memory. "Whenever Schultz realized that the Allied POWs in Stalag 13 were hatching some devious scheme, to stay out of trouble Schultz would pretend ignorance and proclaim, "I know nothing! NOTHING!"

Albert glanced over at Raymond, who was not caught up in the jovial mood of the evening. He asked the young lawyer if everything was all right.

"Hardly," replied Raymond. "I'm sorry, but the story about Sergeant Schultz just didn't seem very funny after what I went through today."

"A bad day in court?" asked Arthur.

"The judge really let me have it," replied Raymond. "I'm defending an insurance company that is being sued by a former employee. The employee alleges that he was a victim of age discrimination. A few weeks ago I had a discovery meeting with the plaintiff's lawyers. I figured that I would do the traditional stonewall routine. After all, if they don't know about something, why would I volunteer it? I don't want them demanding millions of emails and electronic documents and instant messages and memos. I don't have the time or the resources to provide my opponent with evidence against my client."

"Let me guess," said Albert. "They complained to the judge and they cited *Mancia v. Mayflower Textile Services Company.*"

"How did you know?" said Raymond.

Albert smiled. "In 2008 the Federal district court addressed the limits on discovery imposed by the rules of procedure, ethics and statutes, specifically focusing on Fed. R. Civ. P. 26(g). In his decision, Magistrate Judge Paul W. Grimm emphasized that litigants must communicate and cooperate in order to avoid costly and inefficient discovery practices. Although not limited to cases with electronic discovery issues, the application of *Mancia* could prove critical in cases involving large amounts of electronically stored information."

"The court's opinion is well worth reading," added Arthur. "It contains an excellent discussion of the federal rules that require a cooperative approach to discovery. The opinion establishes a solid legal foundation for the new Sedona Conference Cooperation Proclamation, which, in the words of the Proclamation, launches a coordinated effort to promote cooperation by all parties to the discovery process to achieve the goal of a 'just, speedy, and inexpensive determination of every action.'"

"Indeed," said Albert, "*Mancia* shows that far from being a law-school theory, the cooperative approach to discovery is now mandated by the law. As Sedona says, lawyers have two obligations: they are required to advocate for their client but also act as responsible officers of the court. Cooperation does not conflict with the advancement of the client's interests; it enhances it. Only when lawyers confuse *advocacy* with *adversarial conduct* are these twin duties in conflict."

"Saying 'I know nothing' may have worked on *Hogan's Heroes*," said Albert, "But not in today's discovery process."

A few weeks later Arthur saw Raymond on the courthouse steps. "How did you make out with your age discrimination case?"

"Very well, thanks," replied Raymond. "We had a discovery meeting, we agreed on what we would provide, they reviewed the material, we made an offer, they agreed. Case settled! Everybody went home happy."

☑ Simon says: Don't draw discovery sanctions by stonewalling or trying to make discovery overly burdensome. With modern discovery typically involving gigabytes of documents in electronic form, you'd better be using the latest technology to properly identify, preserve, collect, process, review and produce it.

32: The Unavailable Myth
When you're out of the office business will just have to wait

"We've got a nice westerly breeze at five knots," said Fred Glassman. "A perfect day for a sail around the bay! Who's on board?"

At the bar at the Sandy Shore Yacht Club, Arthur Simon and Judd Kessler had been discussing the latest technology. "Count us in," said Arthur.

Liz Lively raised her hand too. "Aye, Aye, captain!"

"I'm afraid I have to pass," moaned Dick Scott.

"Why?" asked Liz. "I thought you had the afternoon off."

"Yes, I did too, but I just checked my voicemail and two clients left messages for me so I've got to get back to the office."

"Can't you handle everything from here?" inquired Liz.

"No, I need to check my calendar to answer one client's question, and the other needs to discuss a document I emailed him. Also, I make it a practice not to talk with clients on my cell phone because it's too hard to track and bill for my time, so I really need to get back to my desk."

"Just hold on a minute, Dick," commanded Arthur. "Judd, would you be so kind as to share with my friend Dick here how you freed me from my desk?"

"I'd be delighted," responded Judd. "With his trusty smart phone, Arthur is virtually in his office wherever he goes. We can be a mile offshore on Fred's lovely forty-foot sailboat and if anyone needs Arthur they can get him instantly by voice, text, or email."

"Yeah, but what about checking his calendar, accessing documents, and billing for his time?" pressed Dick.

"I can do all that too!" exclaimed Arthur. "Judd got me set up so my calendar is automatically synchronized with my smart phone. I can have any document emailed to me so I can read it on my phone. Or, I can use the phone's web browser to access my office computer remotely. And, after every call a little window pops up for me to pick the client and matter and a bill slip for my time is created that magically appears on our office billing system."

Dick's head was already spinning and he wasn't even on board. "That is unbelievable! I can't believe I've been stuck in the office while you guys can be out here playing!"

"From my laptop in the cabin I can do everything Arthur can," said Fred. "It has a wireless Internet card. I use a remote desktop connection into my computer at my desk in the office. It's just like being there."

"That's all well and good, but do you really want clients calling you on your cell phone all the time?" asked Dick.

"Actually," replied Fred, "I just give clients my direct dial number at my office. Whenever I don't answer there, my office phone system puts the caller on hold while it finds me at my home office or my cell phone. I can see the caller ID and either pick up the call or let it go to voicemail. Any voicemail is automatically emailed to me as a wave file that I can click on and listen to on my laptop. Come on board, I'll show you!"

An hour later the group was on the boat, enjoying the view of the shoreline from the blue expanse of the bay. "I think I see my house!" said Liz. "Up there on the hill – that red roof."

Fred called Dick down into the cabin. "Let me show you this," he said, taking a seat in front of his laptop. "I'm looking at my calendar back at the office. I just checked it and I see that the client meeting that had been set for five o'clock has been postponed until tomorrow morning. I also have a revised document to approve before the meeting, and I see that our motion for dismissal has been approved by the judge. Not bad for a day spent sailing on the bay!"

"That's fantastic, Fred," replied Dick. "Judd, can you help me get set up like Fred and Arthur?"

"Absolutely," agreed Judd, "as soon as we get back on dry land!"

☑ Simon says: Unchain yourself from your desk. With the right technology you can conduct business from anywhere. Delight clients by taking their calls and handling matters while you easily bill for hours of extra time when you're out of the office.

33: The Happy Client Myth

A good result guarantees a happy client

"Did I ever tell you the story about that painting?" said Arthur Simon. He was seated in the lounge of the University Club with Georgia Billings, waiting for her law partner Dick Scott to arrive.

"Which one?" asked Georgia, as she sipped her Manhattan.

"The scene over the bar," replied Arthur. "Ten years ago one of our members, Gabe Grumpus, was serving on the University Club redecorating committee. One day he went to an antiques dealer and saw the painting. He suspected it was a work by John Sloan, the noted Ashcan School artist, even though the dealer said it was by a lesser artist. So Gabe paid a couple of hundred bucks for the painting and the dealer was thrilled to have made the sale. Gabe took the painting to an art expert. Sure enough old Gabe was right – it's an authentic John Sloan, and worth six figures. The dealer found out and suddenly he wasn't thrilled anymore. He sued the club. Of course he lost in court, and ever since then we've had an Ashcan School masterpiece hanging behind the bar."

"Good for Gabe," groused Georgia. "Maybe he can work a similar miracle at my law firm."

"Why? What's the problem?" asked Arthur.

"A few months ago I handled a very tough easement dispute between two property owners in Malibu. My client was a millionaire art gallery owner for whom I'd done work in the past. He thought he was entitled to access to the beach over the other guy's property. There was a lot of back and forth negotiations before we finally arrived at a fair resolution. Everyone was happy, or so I thought."

"It's the 'happy' clients that you have to be wary of," cautioned Arthur. "When one turns on you, it's out of the blue, you never see it coming, and you realize that you had let down your guard and didn't do the things you would have done to protect yourself if you didn't think you were dealing with a happy client."

"Oh yes, you're dead on with that one, Arthur," agonized Georgia. "So after the deal is all signed, sealed and delivered, my client's wife gets involved. She's convinced that he got screwed and that I was to blame, so now he is suing me for malpractice."

"Happiness is relative," sighed Arthur. "What seems equitable today can seem unfair tomorrow. That's why it's so important to have a system in place to document every contact with a client. You have a system for that, don't you?"

"Well, sort of," responded Georgia. "I usually jot down notes on a pad I keep beside the phone, and at the end of the day try to remember exactly what was discussed when I input my time entries into our billing system, so I've got some of the history there."

"That's a little backwards, isn't it?" asked Arthur.

"What do you mean?" replied Georgia.

"With the right technology, every time you're on the phone, you can review all the past notes, emails, documents on the matter, on screen, and simultaneously take new notes as you're discussing the matter. As soon as you're done with the call, you just click a button to create the bill slip with those notes, which of course you can edit as needed."

Georgia had a quizzical look on her face. Arthur continued, "Memories morph over minutes. When you make it a regular practice to note the questions, answers, issues, and decisions at the moment of contact with each party, you'll be protecting yourself. Your notes create a chronology which is a great memory refresher later that makes it very hard to dispute what actually occurred. That can be critical when you review with the client, and in this case his wife, what was known at the time, the risks presented, and the decision that were made."

"So I could possibly be avoiding this whole malpractice mess just by reviewing with my client and his wife what our conversations were, including notes on the negotiations with the other side, and why he was smart to settle at the time," concluded Georgia.

Arthur raised his glass. "Here's a toast to a lesson learned and hopes that you won't have to face it again."

As Georgia and Arthur clinked glasses Georgia promised, "Arthur, tomorrow I'm implementing the technology you recommend so I never have to worry about this sort of thing again."

☑ Simon says: If you don't have an easy system for tracking every contact with every party, you may find it difficult to convince the 'happy client' that she shouldn't sue you for malpractice, or unprepared to defend yourself when she does.

34: The Great Lawyer Myth
Potential clients will wait for a great lawyer to call them back

One afternoon Gunter Enz and Arthur Simon were visiting the RMS *Titanic* exhibit at the local museum. "Isn't it amazing," remarked Gunter, "that it was the RMS *Carpathia* that came to the rescue of the *Titanic* and its passengers."

"What was so amazing?" replied Arthur. "The wireless operator on the *Carpathia* heard the distress call from the *Titanic* and immediately the *Carpathia* steamed to the rescue."

"Ah, but there was another ship that was even closer to the *Titanic*. As the *Titanic* sank, this vessel was within viewing distance."

"Extraordinary! What was the name of this ship? Why didn't it come to the rescue?"

"The ship was the SS *Californian*. At half-past midnight on the morning of April 15, 1912, the *Californian's* wireless officer, Cyril Evans, turned off his wireless and went to bed. Ten minutes later the *Titanic*, which was visible on the horizon, struck the iceberg. The *Titanic's* wireless operator sent a general SOS. The *Californian* never heard the distress call because their wireless was shut down. Sixty miles away, the *Carpathia's* wireless operator, Harold Cottam, was at his post. He picked up the signal and the *Carpathia* steamed to the rescue."

"So if Cyril Evans had stayed by his wireless for another half-hour, history would have been changed. Instead, it was Harold Cottam who was the hero."

Just then they were joined by Julie Frick of Frick & Frack. "Hello Arthur and Gunter," she said. "Enjoying the *Titanic* exhibit? It's making me depressed. It reminds me too much of my practice."

"Why, is something the matter?" asked Arthur.

"Look at this," said Julie as she handed Arthur the morning paper.

The headline read "Sally Rich in Sensational Divorce." The story quoted Rich's attorney, Mr. Big Gunz from the firm of Axel, Gunz & Rose.

"Big bucks for Big Gunz," said Arthur.

"Big bucks that should have been coming to us," said Julie. "This morning our receptionist Krystal suddenly remembered that Sally Rich called last week. It was during lunch, and no one was around. At the time, Krystal assumed that if Rich wanted to hire a lawyer she would call back."

"But she hired Axel, Gunz & Rose."

"Welcome to the jungle," said Arthur. "In today's competitive environment you need to engage every prospect on the first call. Clients are often stressed and feel a sense of urgency, and when they need a lawyer they start dialing from the top of a list. They often hire the first lawyer who takes the time to hear their story. Krystal didn't take the time to hear Sally Rich's story, and so the soon-to-be-wealthy-divorcée took her business elsewhere."

Julie rubbed her temples with her fingertips. "What can I do besides provide more training for Krystal?"

"If the client thinks their issue is an emergency, it's an emergency," said Gunter. "A survey conducted by LawInfo found that 86% of people who are contacting an attorney for the first time and get voicemail will hang up and move on to the next attorney on the list. Here's a true story: two of LawInfo's Lead Counsel Program attorneys in Cincinnati were sitting together at lunch. The first attorney received a call on his cell phone and he let it go to voicemail. Within a minute, the other attorney received a call, which he answered, and set an appointment. When the first attorney got back to his office after lunch and returned the voicemail, it was too late. That's when he learned that the call his colleague took at lunch was from the same prospect!"

"Marketing in the twenty-first century is about instant gratification," added Arthur.

"That's right," said Gunter. "We also found that 74% of potential clients expect a 24-hour response time and 26% expect a response in 12 hours. Being accessible gives you a competitive advantage that clients love and will reward with referrals. In fact, the attorney a client speaks to first will usually get their business."

Arthur explained that his firm had recently purchased phone messaging software that had dramatically improved the firm's ability to respond to incoming calls. When a call comes in, the contact details are recorded into the contacts database along with a resolution of the call, such as if it was a wrong number or a potential client. Marketing reports were then easy to generate.

"Ideally, a live person should always answer your phone during business hours," said Gunter. "If it can't be you, it should be a friendly and knowledgeable staff person. While you may think clients don't care about the person who answers the phone, this is wrong. The person answering the phone represents you. After all, you never get a second chance to make a first impression."

"Last week a woman called the office and asked a lot of questions, and then she hung up," said Arthur. "I saw the call information and decided to phone her. The only reason she had hung up was because her boss had just walked into the office. The woman wants to file suit against the local school board because her child is being harassed on the school bus. Our first meeting is tomorrow."

"Good luck," said Julie.

"Thanks. It could be nothing, or it could be another *Davis v. Munroe County Board of Education*. You never know."

"And in the future," said Julie, "Frick & Frack will make sure that we follow in the footsteps of Harold Cottam. When we receive a call, we will be ready to respond."

☑ Simon says: In our fast-paced high-tech society, clients seek instant gratification. If you don't take the opportunity to be the first lawyer to talk with a prospect, your competitor will, and there's better than a 90% chance that prospect will become his client. Let technology help you capture and serve more than your fair share of good clients.

35: The Good Lawyering Myth
Good lawyering is the only marketing you need

Closing the door behind them as they entered the office of Pinto & Hawley, Arthur Simon and Larry Kohn stood in the vestibule. The big Victorian house, recently converted to law offices, was usually bustling with activity. But Arthur and Larry heard nothing – no phones ringing, no conversations.

Arthur poked his head into the office of his young friend Charlie Hawley.

"Hello, Arthur, come in," said Charlie. He was seated behind his desk. Spread out in front of him was the morning newspaper.

"Thanks, Charlie. Ready for lunch? Larry and I are headed to the Pullman Diner. Say, it sure is quiet around here."

Charlie shrugged. "I guess we hit a slow period. No new clients. I've got plenty of time for lunch. Let's go."

A few minutes later Larry, Arthur and Charlie settled into one of the red vinyl and chrome booths in the diner, a converted railroad car. They ordered burgers, fries, and coffee.

"Charlie, aren't you concerned about your client flow?" asked Arthur.

"Yes, I am," replied Charlie. "We need to boost revenues. If we don't get more clients we will have to lay off one of our legal assistants. But what can I do? Every law firm experiences a slow period from time to time."

"My friend, you need a reality check. The days of every member of the bar association being guaranteed a comfortable income are over. We live in a competitive environment. You can and should do more to promote the firm, because in the years ahead these slow periods, as you call them, will become increasingly severe."

"What do you mean?"

"Let's start with a history lesson. During most of the twentieth century, lawyers were prohibited from advertising. They got new clients from referrals, walk-ins, and by handing out business cards at train wrecks. But in 1977 the United States Supreme Court ruled in *Bates v. State Bar of Arizona* that lawyers could advertise in the Yellow Pages, newspapers, magazines, on radio and television – pretty much anywhere a fast-food joint could advertise. The American Bar Association promptly weighed in with a set of professional standards for marketing, admonishing lawyers not to make misleading claims or statements. But the game was on, and soon law firms were vying for clients in the open marketplace."

"That's right," said Larry. "Today you need to be proactive and reach out into the marketplace. Everyone else is doing it, and you can't afford to be invisible."

Charlie frowned. "I see the television ads for personal injury law firms. They seem like a hard sell, designed to rake in the clients. I don't want to be a part of that. And besides, it's expensive."

"You don't have to do what they do," Larry responded. "But I still hear the ridiculous belief creeping into the lives of my clients that lawyers shouldn't market themselves. So many lawyers have been told that good lawyering is the only marketing strategy they need to become successful."

"That's exactly what I've always been told," admitted Charlie.

"Well, it's absurd," continued Larry, "and yet it is easy to believe if you are skeptical about your ability to become a rainmaker. Good lawyers who don't want to market find comfort in the notion that it is lawyering – not marketing – that will build their practice. Good lawyering may result in media exposure and in happy clients telling others about you. And some areas of work provide exposure to new prospects naturally. If you represent a seller, you may meet the buyer. But it is a bad idea to limit your rainmaking to doing good work.

"The truth is that good lawyering alone is usually very slow compared to a structured, strategic rainmaking effort. Speaking, writing, producing events, belonging to the local Chamber of Commerce, Rotary Club, or non-profit organization and becoming a visible member of the community, and inviting people to lunch brings you into contact with more targets. And the more quality targets you meet, the more business you can expect to generate."

The waitress cleared the lunch plates and dessert was ordered. "Remember, Charlie, clients aren't clairvoyant," advised Arthur. "If no one knows about you, no one will hire you."

Charlie nodded. "Okay, I get it. If I don't blow my own horn, nobody will."

"That's right!" said Larry. "You're too good a lawyer not to have clients. Now let's try some of this delicious apple pie."

☑ Simon says: No, the world won't beat a path to your door when you build a better mousetrap. The lawyers preceding you were trapped by tradition and prevented from advertising. But all that has changed. In today's competitive environment the lawyers who've mastered marketing are the ones growing their practices. Do what they're doing. Remember, it's the second mouse that gets the cheese.

About the Authors

Brian Crozier Whitaker, Esq.

A pioneer in providing unbundled self-help legal services, Brian Whitaker provides his clients exactly the legal help they want at an affordable fixed fee. Based in San Diego, California, Brian is the founder and senior partner of Lifeline Legal, LLP, which offers clients fast, low cost help with bankruptcy, divorce and loan modifications.

Mr. Whitaker is admitted to the California State Bar, California Supreme Court, U.S. District Court and United States Bankruptcy Court in the Southern, Central, Eastern and Northern Districts of California. He is a member of the National Association of Consumer Bankruptcy Attorneys and the San Diego County Bar and Bankruptcy Forum.

A graduate of the University of Chicago, Mr. Whitaker earned his JD at the Western State University College of Law.

Brian Whitaker may be contacted at lifelinelegal.com or at lawmyths.com.

Gunter Enz

Since 1994, Gunter Enz, CEO and founder of LawInfo, has been a leader in providing the public with free online legal resources and access to pre-qualified, pre-screened attorneys. Recognized nationwide as one of the top three Internet legal portals, LawInfo has become an invaluable marketing resource for law firms who want to produce qualified leads from the Internet.

LawInfo's signature service, the Lead Counsel Program, was designed to provide a simple and reliable way for anyone on the Web to find a pre-qualified, pre-screened attorney quickly and easily. Lead Counsel Members must earn the right to use the Lead Counsel designation by passing a certification process which includes peer recommendations, bar checks, and minimum practice area experience.

Gunter Enz may be contacted at lawinfo.com or at lawmyths.com.

Michael W. Quade, Esq.

With a reputation as a vigorous client advocate and outstanding trial lawyer, Michael Quade has won verdicts in excess of seven figures and handled civil cases as varied as assault and battery, insurance bad faith, contract disputes with car dealerships and construction defects. As the founder of Quade & Associates in San Diego, California, Mr. Quade has appeared and argued in both State and Federal Courts as well as before the 9th Circuit Court of Appeals.

Prior to founding his own law firm, he specialized in insurance defense and construction defect litigation. Mr. Quade earned a mechanical engineering degree from San Diego State University and his JD from National University. A native Californian who continues to enjoy living in the sunshine state, he is passionate about the practice of the law, and when he is not preparing for trial he enjoys skiing, and soccer and basketball with his kids.

Michael Quade may be contacted at quadelaw.com or lawmyths.com.

Albert Barsocchini, Esq.

As Senior Director and Assistant General Counsel for Guidance Software, Mr. Barsocchini advises corporate, government, and law enforcement organizations in advanced eDiscovery and digital investigations. Based in Pasadena, California, Guidance Software is a world leader in assisting its clients in conducting thorough and effective computer investigations.

In addition to his in-house legal responsibilities, Mr. Barsocchini works with corporate and public sector law departments seeking to implement defensible and cost-efficient in-house eDiscovery processes.

Mr. Barsocchini writes and speaks regularly in the United States and Asia on eDiscovery, digital investigations, and the intersection between law and technology. His numerous articles and books include *Attorney's Guide to the Internet* (CEB Book). He currently serves as a Special Master for the State Bar of California and for litigants in the California State Courts.

Prior to joining Guidance Software, Mr. Barsocchini was a trial attorney. He served as Chairman of the State Bar of California Law

Practice Management & Technology Section, was a founding member of the California State Bar Cyberspace Law Committee and was a legal consultant for Thomson West.

Albert Barsocchini may be contacted at guidancesoftware.com or lawmyths.com.

Lawrence Kohn

Through effective coaching, Larry Kohn turns ordinary lawyers into powerful rainmakers. The founder and president of Kohn Communications, Larry has personally conducted over 26,000 individual consultations with professionals and executives. The Los Angeles, California-based firm helps its clients to increase profitability by improving their communication skills in marketing and management.

Mr. Kohn is known as an informative, entertaining, and dynamic speaker who regularly appears at law firms and trade organizations nationwide. A successful writer, he is the co-author of *Selling With Honor: Strategies For Selling Without Selling Your Soul* (Penguin/Putnam, 1997), *Selling In Your Comfort Zone* (American Bar Association, 2009) and "Marketing Through the Spoken Word," which appears in *The Complete Guide to Marketing Your Law Practice* (American Bar Association, 1999). Larry has authored many articles appearing in the monthly newsletter of the Law Practice Management & Technology Section of the State Bar of California.

A graduate of the University of Southern California where he was the president of Zeta Beta Tau fraternity, for over 20 years Mr. Kohn was a Master Instructor at UCLA Extension, teaching marketing, communications, and public speaking.

Larry Kohn may be reached at kohncommunications.com or at lawmyths.com.

Thomas A. Hauck

Having delighted readers with his writing of everything from fiction to financial news, Tom Hauck's services include ghostwriting books; writing financial newsletters, web copy, and white papers; and editing scholarly reports. His background in nonprofit makes him much sought after for help with grant writing and major fundraising campaigns. Based in Gloucester, Massachusetts, Tom is also the editor of *Renaissance Magazine*, a bimonthly national glossy.

Tom's recently released *Pistonhead* is a novel about Charlie Sinclair, a guy who plays guitar in a metal band at night while working in a factory by day. Upcoming releases will include a book of short stories and poetry, followed by a horror thriller.

A graduate of Tufts University with a BA in History of Art, Mr. Hauck earned his MBA at Endicott College.

Tom Hauck may be reached at thomashauck.net or lawmyths.com.

Judd Kessler, Esq.

Since 1983, Judd Kessler, founder and president of Abacus Data Systems, Inc. and developer of AbacusLaw software, has helped hundreds of thousands of lawyers in over 60 countries create the law practice of their dreams.

Mr. Kessler served as Chairman of the State Bar of California Law Practice Management & Technology Section. He is a featured speaker at bar associations throughout the country, and has authored numerous articles and books including *The Attorney's Guide to the Internet* (CEB Book).

After earning his degree in economics and computer science from the University of California San Diego at age nineteen, Judd went on to become one of the youngest real estate brokers and general contractors in the state. Since then he has started and grown over a dozen successful businesses and is always happy to share his secrets of success with others.

When he's not working, Judd enjoys a challenging game of tennis or piloting his Citation jet around the country.

Judd Kessler may be contacted at abacuslaw.com or lawmyths.com.

FORTUNEHOUSE
PUBLISHERS

Fortunehouse Publishers •Box E •Rancho Santa Fe, CA 92067